A LIFE OF INTEGRITY

A LIFE OF INTEGRITY

*13 Outstanding Leaders Raise the Standard
for Today's Christian Men*

HOWARD HENDRICKS
GENERAL EDITOR

MULTNOMAH BOOKS

SISTERS, OREGON

A LIFE OF INTEGRITY
published by Multnomah Publishers, Inc.

© 1997 by Multnomah Publishers, Inc.

International Standard Book Number: 1-57673-136-7

Cover illustration by Left Coast Design

Printed in the United States of America

Unless otherwise noted, Scripture quotations are from:
The Holy Bible, New International Version (NIV) © 1973, 1984 by
International Bible Society, used by permission of Zondervan Publishing House

Also quoted:
New American Standard Bible (NASB)
© 1960, 1977 by the Lockman Foundation

Scripture quotations marked "NKJV" are taken from the New King James Version.
Copyright © 1979, 1980, 1982 by Thomas Nelson, Inc.
Used by permission. All rights reserved.

The King James Version (KJV)

The Living Bible (TLB) © 1971 by Tyndale House Publishers

The New Revised Standard Version Bible (NRSV)
© 1989 by the Division of Christian Education
of the National Council of the Churches of Christ
in the United States of America

The New Testament in Modern English, Revised Edition (Phillips)
© 1972 by J. B. Phillips

Excerpt from article by Peggy Noonan reprinted by permission of
Forbes magazine ©Forbes Inc., 1992.

For information:
MULTNOMAH PUBLISHERS, INC.
POST OFFICE BOX 1720
SISTERS, OREGON 97759

Library of Congress Cataloging-in-Publication Data
A man of integrity: 13 outstanding leaders raise the standard for today's Christian
men/Howard Hendricks. general editor. p.cm.   ISBN 1-57673-136-7 (alk. paper)
 1. Men--Religious life. 2. Men (Christian theology) I. Hendricks, Howard G.
BV4528.2.M315   1997   96-40127
248.8'42--dc21   CIP
            01 02 03 04 05 — 7 6 5 4 3 2

CONTENTS

ACKNOWLEDGMENTS

This book was the brainchild of my good friend John Van Diest, who pushed and prodded and made sure we got all the right people on all the right topics. Without him, this project would have never gotten off the ground.

I would also like to thank the Promise Keeper speakers who participated in creating this text. They've all written books, and no doubt will write more, so I'm glad they agreed to share their best stuff within these pages.

Finally, while I am proud to serve as General Editor of this tome, the real credit belongs to the very gifted Chip MacGregor, who seems to keep stepping in to help me at just the right time. Thanks, Chip!

INTRODUCTION

Years ago I knew an elderly lady who really loved the Lord and was always challenging me to love Him more. We used to run into each other at conferences, and she would ask me something like "Well, Hendricks, what's the best book you've read in the last year?" or "What answer to prayer have you experienced lately?" One of my fondest memories is seeing her on a tour of the Holy Land with a bunch of big NFL players—she was out in front of them, yelling, "Come *on,* men! Let's get with it!"

I love that sort of spirit, and, to be honest, there are times I need someone like that spurring me on. An encouraging word (or even a kick in the pants) can be remarkably invigorating. I think you'll find this book does the same thing. There are words here from men who ought to be in the "hall of fame" for Christians. Men like Bill Bright, who started the world's second-largest Christian organization, and Luis Palau, who has probably spoken to more people about Christ than anybody except Billy Graham. You'll find words here from some experts: Dennis Rainey on marriage, and Ron Blue on money. You'll also find encouragement and practical suggestions from guys like John Maxwell and Bruce Wilkinson. Every one an expert in his field, and every one sharing from the heart on how we can become men of integrity.

So don't just buy this book and let it sit on your coffee table. Pick it up and read a chapter. Talk through the study questions with a friend. Decide to take one of the principles and apply it to your life, and ask a friend to hold you accountable to do so. We've had enough "pie in the sky" material. Here you'll find practical lessons from Promise Keeper speakers on how to develop integrity in your life, your marriage, your family, and your world. As my friend would say, "Come on, man! Get with it!"

CHAPTER ONE

COMMITTED
TO THE KING

LUIS PALAU

God is accomplishing a great work in America today. You can see His presence everywhere. There's the men's movement. There are the marches for Jesus. There are the concerts of prayer. Christian radio and television are more popular than ever. Churches and entire denominations are beginning to work together, rather than remain apart. There is an excitement about standing for the Lord. God is at work in our society.

One of the greatest evidences of that is the pull back toward biblical manhood, fostered by Promise Keepers and other Christian men's organizations. We are not a bunch of angry males, getting together to exclude others. We are *for* biblical manhood. We support racial oneness in Jesus Christ. We are for servant leadership. We love our wives, we love our daughters, and we love our daughters-in-law. We are part of this movement because we are for the gospel and Jesus Christ, wanting to live holy lives for His cause. The only thing we are against is sin in our personal lives. That's what we want to change. If we're going to make an impact on our world, the first thing we must consider is how we can strengthen our commitment to Christ.

In the days of the Roman Empire, Caesar had people go ahead of him and bow before him, burning incense and saying, "Caesar is lord. Caesar is lord." Refusing to say it was considered treason and could lead to death. But the Christians came along, and they said, "No. Caesar is not lord. Jesus is Lord." Those words brought revolution to the Roman Empire. Imagine what impact a million godly men could have in America if we were to stand up and say, "Jesus is Lord."

You see, God is the King of kings. He is the Lord who reigns over us. You've probably been in a service and sung the words, "Blessed be the Lord God Almighty, who reigns forevermore." But does Jesus Christ reign over your life? Does He control your life? I believe that's the big question in America today.

THE KING

Luke 19 tells the story of people who knew of the king but wouldn't acknowledge him. Luke tells us that the people in Jesus' time thought the kingdom of God was going to appear at once. So the Lord said to them, "A man of noble birth went to a distant country to have himself appointed king and then to return. So he called ten of his servants and gave them ten minas. 'Put this money to work,' he said, 'until I come back.' But his subjects hated him and sent a delegation after him to say, 'We don't want this man to be our king.' He was made king, however, and returned home" (Luke 19:12–15). Jesus Christ is King, whether we want to admit it or not. A strong commitment to the King is essential if we're going to be part of changing our world.

I have four sons. Three of them have walked with the Lord since they were little kids. The twins, who are the oldest, were converted when they were little boys, were baptized, and went on in their commitment to Jesus Christ. They both attended a Christian college and married good Christian girls, and they're doing great. It was the same with my fourth boy.

But my third son, Andrew, who is a tall, handsome kid (just like his dad), got offtrack at some point in his commitment to Christ. His mother and I began to pray for him. In high school, he never denied the gospel or turned against Jesus Christ or blasphemed the Bible. He just took off on his own way. He went to the University of Oregon, joined a fraternity, and didn't walk with God. After graduation he was off to Boston, and I tell you my wife and I used to cry for that boy. We used to pray for him hours on end.

I do crusades, and sometimes I'd be in a country preaching, giving the invitation to come to Jesus Christ, and thousands of young people would come. I would look at them in front of me and I'd cry. My son wasn't among them. "Lord," I would say, "when is Andrew coming home?" You can lead thousands into the kingdom, but if one of your boys isn't in the kingdom, it breaks your heart.

A couple of years ago we were in Jamaica. We had a huge crowd, and in the audience was my son Andrew. A businessman gave his testimony, a Jewish guy who had committed his life to Christ, and at the end of his message, I preached. The whole time I was praying for my son. That night in the hotel room my wife and I were packing our bags because it was the last day of the crusade, when suddenly there was a knock on our door. It was one o'clock in the morning, and there was our son Andrew. He came running into the room, jumped on the bed, and said, "Dad, Mom, I'm back." That night he recommitted his life to Christ. Later he married the daughter of the businessman who gave the testimony that night, and he completed graduate work at a biblical seminary in Portland, Oregon. He's found happiness and fulfillment in his commitment to Christ. What a change in his life!

You may be in a similar situation. You may not be sure if you're a Christian. Or perhaps you used to be close to the Lord, but you've allowed yourself to move away from Him. Your dad may be a preacher, your parents may be godly, and your in-laws may be leaders in the church, but you've drifted away from God. Yet inside, you know the Lord is King. Jesus is saying to you, "I want to be king of your life. I want to be the master. I want to run your life." You can be like those people in Luke 19 who chose to reject the king, or you can decide to be committed to Christ.

RULER OVER YOUR MIND

So the first thing I want to ask you is this: "Does God rule over your intellect?"

Before you go any farther in reading how to live as a godly man, let me ask you, "Does God reign over your mind? Who do you go to when you're looking for answers? Who do you go to for doctrine, for spiritual issues? Have you submitted your intellect to God Almighty?"

Early in His ministry, Jesus had huge crowds following Him around. It was easy to be close to the King. But Jesus once said to His disciples, "Unless you eat the flesh of the Son of Man and drink his blood, you have no life in you" (John 6:53). At that, everybody began to drift away. And Jesus turned to His disciples and asked, "Do you also want to go away?" Peter said, "Lord, to whom shall we go? You have the words of eternal life" (see John 6:60–68). Peter recognized that you can't take just *part* of Jesus. If you want to be saved, you must commit your whole life to Him.

Have you submitted your mind to Jesus Christ? Does God rule over your intellect? Do you take the Word of God seriously and say, "Lord, to whom can I go? You have the words of eternal life"?

RULER OVER YOUR MORALS

Second, let me ask you, "Does God reign over your morals?"

In America today, talking about holiness seems old-fashioned. Are you a godly man? We like to sing about being godly, but sometimes I wonder how many are really willing to make that commitment. To be a godly man doesn't mean you'll be perfect but that you'll become an honest man who walks in the light with God. "Be holy, because I am holy," says the Lord (Leviticus 11:44). Are you a holy man? Do you walk with God?

The Book of Hebrews warns us to "pursue peace with all men, and holiness, without which no one will see the Lord" (Hebrews 12:14, NKJV). Jesus is our standard of holiness. The Lord was pure toward women, and we must be also. As men, we have to face the fact that it isn't just high school kids or college students who have a problem with morals. Many men in America struggle with keeping godly morals. As Christians, we need to develop a holy attitude toward women, where we honor our wives and where our commitment to Christ controls our morality.

Is Jesus Christ God over your sexuality? Have you put your sexuality under the control of the King? I've been living for the Lord many years. I'm not a kid anymore—I'm a grandpa—and I'm an evangelist, but temptations still come at me. I've had to put my sexuality under the control of Jesus Christ. If you're struggling with pornography or homosexuality or fantasizing, and you can't break the hold of sexuality over your life, you have to commit it to the Lord. He says, "My son, give me your heart." Jesus can set you free from slavery to the passions of sex. It isn't that sex goes away, or that temptation no longer attacks you, but that your morality is under the Lordship of Jesus Christ.

While I was at a missions conference in Urbana, Illinois, with seventeen thousand college students, one of the leaders came to me and said, "Luis, there's a guy, a football player, with a butcher knife! He's about to kill himself!" So I went to his dorm room, and here was this massive running back for the University of Illinois, knife in hand, threatening to end his life. I asked everybody to leave the room, and then I said, "Why are you trying to kill yourself?"

And he replied, "Louie, I'm not worthy to be alive."

"Why aren't you worthy to be alive?"

"I have a perverted mind. I spend my life alone. I want to go out with women, but I'm too cowardly. I sing in the church choir, and instead of singing I'm looking at women and coveting the whole bunch of them." Then he picked up the knife and added, "So I'm going to kill myself."

I don't think he was really going to kill himself, but he did feel totally unworthy to be alive. His thought life enslaved him. He was out of control. But that night he gave control of his life to Jesus Christ.

Is Jesus the Lord over your morals? If we're going to make an impact on our world for the cause of Christ, we've got to allow Christ to change our minds and our morals. Commit your morality to Him. Just say, "Lord Jesus, come and take control of my morals. I want to live in holiness. I want to be a godly man." Commit yourself to Jesus Christ.

RULER OVER YOUR WILL

The third question I want to ask you is "Does God rule over your will?" Do you obey the Lord, even when it is hard to do so? Some of the men in Christ's parable did. Back in Luke 19, we read these words:

> "Then he sent for the servants to whom he had given the money, in order to find out what they had gained with it.
>
> "The first one came and said, 'Sir, your mina has earned ten more.'
>
> "'Well done, my good servant!' his master replied. 'Because you have been trustworthy in a very small matter, take charge of ten cities.'

"The second came and said, 'Sir, your mina has earned five more.'

"His master answered, 'You take charge of five cities.'

"Then another servant came and said, 'Sir, here is your mina; I have kept it laid away in a piece of cloth. I was afraid of you, because you are a hard man. You take out what you did not put in and reap what you did not sow.'

"His master replied, 'I will judge you by your own words, you wicked servant! You knew, did you, that I am a hard man, taking out what I did not put in, and reaping what I did not sow? Why then didn't you put my money on deposit, so that when I came back, I could have collected it with interest?'

"Then he said to those standing by, 'Take his mina away from him and give it to the one who has ten minas.'

"'Sir,' they said, 'he already has ten!'

"He replied, 'I tell you that to everyone who has, more will be given, but as for the one who has nothing, even what he has will be taken away. But those enemies of mine who did not want me to be king over them—bring them here and kill them in front of me.'" (Luke 19:15–27)

Some of those servants were afraid, but willing to obey. Others were unwilling to obey. They were uncommitted to the king. Are you committed enough to obey? Are you afraid of talking about Jesus? Are you ashamed of the Lord? He said, "Whoever has my commands and obeys them, he is the one who loves me. He who loves me will be loved by my Father, and I too will love him and show myself to him" (John 14:21).

If your will needs to be under the control of Christ, commit yourself to Jesus Christ and say, "Lord Jesus, I want to be obedient, but I need the power of the Holy Spirit." The power of God can come on your life and enable you to keep your commitments. Notice what Jesus said about those fellows in His parable: They were to get to work. The master left gifts with them, expecting them to work. All, except one, went and did their job. They showed their commitment to the king, and He responded with the words, "Well done, my good servant. Because you've been faithful over little, I will put you over much." The servants who obeyed were commended and given more. Faithfulness in the Christian life is a result of Jesus being King of your life, ruling over your life. It is the product of obedience, and obedience comes from commitment.

Think about your family. Does God rule over your family life? Do your family members see the hand print of God in your life? I was reading a *Newsweek* magazine the other day, in which there was an article about the problem of fathers in America. The article was titled, "Dear dads, save your sons." Too many dads aren't setting an example of commitment to their sons. The boys don't know what their fathers believe. Does God rule over your family life?

God, our Heavenly Father, loves your family. The Lord loves that woman He gave you. He loves those boys He gave you. He loves those girls He gave you. You may be thinking, "Luis, I made a mistake. I married the wrong woman. She isn't the kind of woman I really want." But God knows all about your family. He worked it all out in His mysterious way, brought her to you, and believes she is best for you. So we've got to commit to our wives, as God's perfect gift to us.

The Bible says "the husband is the head of the wife," so we've got to commit to being godly husbands to our wives. Ephesians chapter five says that we are to love our wives "as Christ loved the church and gave himself up for her" (5:25). It takes commitment to love your wife as much as Christ loves the church. The Bible also says that God gave you a wife so you could bring godly offspring into the world (Malachi 2:15). That means we fathers have to be committed to our children. We not only bring those boys and girls into the world, we are supposed to train them so they become godly.

Our world is in trouble. America is in trouble because Jesus Christ is not the God of America. He is no longer King. We've decided, like those foolish men in Christ's parable, that "we don't want this man to be king over us." Brothers, we've got to bring Jesus back as King of the United States of America. If we really want our nation to change, that's what is needed. God has planted you as a man in your family and said to you, "I want you to reflect My Son, Jesus Christ." It's time we commit to doing that. Then when your woman looks at you, with all your faults and all your failures, she can say, "This old boy that Jesus gave me is okay. This guy reflects Jesus, and I love him, even if he's out of shape. I love him because he reflects Jesus Christ to me." Isn't that the kind of man you want to be?

COMMITTED TO THE KING

Brother, are you committed to the Lord? You may claim, "Luis, I want Jesus to be in control of my life, but I don't have time in the morning for prayer and Bible reading before I go to the office." But that's what it will take for your commitment to really reflect the Lord. You can't be like Him unless you spend time with Him.

So right now, you need to say, "Lord, I want You in my life. I want You in my home. I want You in control of my mind and my morals. I want to commit myself to You." You may have drifted from the Lord, like my son Andrew. You may have gone away from the things of God. You haven't denied Jesus Christ perhaps, but you've walked in the ways of sin, you've gone into the world, you've been a coward about Jesus, and you wonder if God will ever take you back. When my son Andrew came back, he told me, "Dad, I went with a bunch of young people up to the hills of Jamaica, and I began to confess my sins. You know, for three hours I just bawled and bawled, and I told the Lord all the junk I'd done. I told Him everything. I wanted it off my chest. I wanted Jesus to take over." Then my son told me, "When it was over, I knew my sins were gone. I was clean in the eyes of God, and I began to sing to the Lord Jesus Christ. I'm committed to Him."

To be King of your life, Jesus died on a cross. He paid with His own blood, allowing Himself to be crucified. They put nails in His hands and His feet. They put a crown of thorns on His head. The Bible says they spit on Him, they slapped Him around, they took off His clothes and made fun of Him. And Jesus didn't say a word. Then when He hung on the cross, He cried out, "My

God! My God! Why have you forsaken Me?" And the answer was "For the people you love so much." For the people of America. Jesus was crucified for you and for me, and He is asking for our wholehearted commitment to Him.

You may think to yourself, "Oh, if you only knew the sins I've committed! God could never forgive me." You may be like that kid in Urbana, Illinois, thinking you are not worthy to be alive. Maybe you've done such shameful things you think God could never forgive you. But the Bible says, "God demonstrates His own love for us in this: While we were still sinners, Christ died for us" (Romans 5:8). The writer to the Hebrews says that "the blood of Christ...[will] cleanse our consciences from acts that lead to death, so that we may serve the living God!" (Hebrews 9:14). Jesus can cleanse you. You can start afresh with God if you will bow your knee and say, "Oh, Jesus, I surrender to You. Oh, Jesus, You be the God of my life. Oh, Lord, wash me and clean me white as snow by the blood of Jesus Christ. I commit my life to You." He wants to be King of your life.

Jesus said, "I stand at the door and knock. If anyone hears my voice and opens the door, I will come in and eat with him, and he with me" (Revelation 3:20). When He comes in, He takes over. He becomes the King of your life. So the question is, is He King of your life?

STUDY QUESTIONS

1. What three words would you use to describe the contents of this chapter? Why those words?

2. Do you agree or disagree with this statement: "You've got to serve somebody"? Defend your answer.

3. Read the parable of the minas found in Luke 19:11–27. What thoughts go through your mind after hearing this story?

4. Exactly what do you think God expects you to do to make him ruler over your mind, morals, will, and family life? What interferes with your ability to do that?

5. How have you seen a man demonstrate commitment to Jesus through his attitudes and actions toward his family?

6. How might your life be different if there were a million men in our nation who were truly committed to Jesus? if there were a thousand in your state? a hundred in your community? one in your home?

7. What can you do this week to be that one man in your home who is truly committed to Christ?

CHAPTER TWO

HOLDING ON TO FAITH

Bob Moorehead

A friend of mine told me he had recently visited Australia and spoken with a dark aborigine. That aborigine said to him, "You know, when black people are born, we're black. When we grow up, we're black, and when we get sick, we're black. And when we go out in the sun, we're black. When we're cold, we're black. When we're scared, we're black, and when we die, we're black. But you white men, you've got a problem. When you're born, you're pink. When you grow up, you're white. When you get sick, you're green. When you go out in the sun, you're red. When you're cold, you're blue, and when you're scared, you're yellow. And when you die, you're purple." Then he added, "And you have the gall to call me colored!"

It's thrilling to look around a Promise Keepers conference and see people of every race and background. We are slowly learning that He has made us of one blood. And God is calling us as men to take a stand with brothers of all races to deliver a message to this nation that we need to come back under the sovereign hand of God again in this country.

BROTHERS IN CHRIST

In the early eighties I wrote my "declaration," which the Lord gave to me. It reads:

> I am a part of the fellowship of the unashamed. I have Holy Spirit power. The die has been cast. I've stepped over the line. The decision has been made. I am a disciple of Jesus Christ. I won't look back, let up, slow down, back away, or be still. My past is redeemed, my present makes sense, and my future is secure. I am finished and done with low living, sight walking, small planning, smooth knees, colorless dreams, tame visions, mundane talking, chintzy giving, and dwarfed goals. I no longer need preeminence, prosperity, position, promotions, plaudits, or popularity. I don't have to be right, tops, first, recognized, praised, regarded, or rewarded. I now live by presence, lean by love, love by patience, live by prayer, and labor by His power. My face is set, my gait is fast, my goal is heaven, my road is narrow, my way is rough, my companions few, my Guide reliable, my mission clear. I cannot be bought, compromised, detoured, lured away or turned back, diluted, or delayed anymore. I will not flinch in the face of sacrifice or hesitate in the presence of adversity, negotiate at the table of the enemy or ponder at the pool of popularity anymore. Nor will I meander in the maze of mediocrity. I am a disciple of Jesus Christ. I won't give

up, shut up, let up, or slow up until I've preached up, paid up, prayed up, stored up, and stayed up for the cause of Jesus Christ. I'm a disciple of Jesus. And I must go till He comes, give till I drop, and preach till all know. And when Jesus comes to get His own, He'll have no problem recognizing me. My colors will be clear because I'm a disciple of Jesus Christ.

God is calling His disciples to begin working together as brothers. In Mark 10:17–22 we read:

As Jesus started on his way, a man ran up to him and fell on his knees before him. "Good teacher," he asked, "what must I do to inherit eternal life?"

"Why do you call me good?" Jesus answered. "No one is good—except God alone. You know the commandments: 'Do not murder, do not commit adultery, do not steal, do not give false testimony, do not defraud, honor your father and mother.'"

"Teacher," he declared, "all these I have kept since I was a boy."

Jesus looked at him and loved him. "One thing you lack," he said. "Go, sell everything you have and give to the poor, and you will have treasure in heaven. Then come, follow me."

At this the man's face fell. He went away sad, because he had great wealth.

STAGE ONE: DESPERATION

I believe with all my heart that this incident describes the stages every man goes through. In my own life, I went through these stages. The first one is the stage of desperation. There's not a man who hasn't been there, or soon will be. Ironically, it's that stage where things look good on the outside. This young man had a lot going for him. He went to the right schools. He drove the right car. He wore the clothes with the right labels. He belonged to the right fraternity. He moved in the right circles. He made investments in the right markets. The Bible says he was a ruler. He was important. He had position. He was wealthy. He had everything going for him. All of the trappings were there. All the invitations were there. But something was wrong, because on the inside he was empty. He was missing something desperately, and it drove him to the feet of Jesus.

We need to give this man credit because he came in the right way. The Scriptures say he ran. That's a picture of desperation. He fell at the feet of Jesus. He came humbly. There's no other way to come to Jesus but humbly. And the Bible says he also came with the right question. "What must I do to inherit eternal life?" And he got the right answer. But he made the wrong decision.

This man had everything going for him. Unfortunately, however, he had a lot in the show window but not much in the warehouse. He came saying, "What must I do to inherit eternal life?" This wasn't business as usual. This man was desperate. He wanted life. That's a picture of many people. It's a picture of me many years ago when I had everything going for me and I thought I was successful, but inside something was missing in my life.

STAGE TWO: FRUSTRATION

There's a second stage, the stage of frustration. The rich young ruler was frustrated. In verse 19, Jesus said to him, "You know the commandments: 'Do not murder, do not commit adultery, do not steal, do not give false testimony, do not defraud, honor your father and mother.'" It's interesting that Jesus pointed him to the Law, not because Jesus thought there was life in the Law, but Jesus had to get this man to see what did *not* give life so he would recognize the One who *does* bring life.

Make no mistake about it, there is no abundant life, joyful life, victorious life, or successful life apart from Jesus Christ. We were created to live in Him. We were created to serve and follow Him, and when we're not doing that, we are living contrary to what we were created to do and be. Jesus didn't say, "Keep the commandments." He said, "You *know* the commandments." There are many men today who rely on their good deeds and their good works. I talk to men every week, and I ask them, "What do you think is going to let you into heaven?" Many say, "Well, I try to live a good life. I try to be a good husband. I try to be a good father. I don't cheat. I don't steal." And when I ask them, "How well do you do those things? Do you do them perfectly? One hundred percent?" I usually get this response: "Well, nobody does it 100 percent."

There's a verse in Galatians chapter 3 that says all who rely on the works of law, or all who rely on doing good deeds, are under a curse. For Scripture says, "Cursed is everyone who does not continue to do *everything* written in the Book of the Law" (Galatians 3:10, emphasis mine).

Jesus in His sovereignty said to this man, "You know the commandments." He didn't say, "You need to keep the commandments." What Jesus is implying is that "you know they don't bring you life. They don't bring you joy. They don't bring you fulfillment. They don't bring you satisfaction."

Many people today are simply manicuring their morals. In desperation and frustration they are simply rearranging the deck chairs on the *Titanic*. What's the use? It's going down. Someone has said that no arrangement of bad eggs will ever make a good omelet. And no matter how many times we move around all the key players in our life, it's not going to solve the problem. The solution is not there. Jesus Christ alone is the answer to our needs. Jesus Christ alone can forgive your horrible past. Jesus Christ alone can bring meaning to your present. Jesus Christ alone can give hope for your future. Nobody else can.

I read about a young staffer in the White House who moved his desk into the men's rest room. Somebody came in and asked, "George, what in the world are you doing with your desk in the men's rest room?" His response was "I have found this is the only place where people really know what they're doing."

It could be true! People are confused. I just finished reading a book about the days of the flower children in San Francisco. As a businessman was walking down the street, he saw a long-haired hippie strumming on a guitar. One chord. The same chord. Many times. Hum, hum, hum. Curious, the man walked over to this hippie and said, "I don't understand. You hit the same chord every time. The other people in the park are going up and down the necks of their guitars, but you hit the same chord every time." The hippie looked up at him and said, "The problem with them is that they're still looking for it. I've found it."

Christian, we have found it in Jesus Christ. He's our all in all. He's the lily of the valley, the bright and Morning Star. He's the one who, someday at the trumpet blast, is going to come back, and He's going to take the church out of this world. He's going to draw all of human history together. And so in this little window of time between now and then, we need to seek first the kingdom of God and His righteousness.

Like the rich young ruler, so many people today are searching for meaning. They didn't find it in illicit sex. They didn't find it in that affair. They didn't find it in that business deal that put them in a six-digit income. They didn't find it in position. They didn't find it in all the titles and the success. And so they keep looking. I'll tell you, though, when you have found Jesus Christ and have invited Him in to be your Lord and Savior, you have found it all. You have found everything.

STAGE THREE: SALVATION

The final stage is what I call the stage of salvation. Jesus looked at that rich young ruler and loved him. "'One thing you lack,' he said.

'Go, sell everything you have and give to the poor, and you will have treasure in heaven. Then come, follow me.'" Many people think Jesus was really saying, "Well, you know, if you can just develop unselfishness in your life, you've found it."

I don't think that's what Jesus was saying. Jesus was telling this man, "You lack one thing in your life, and it's faith in me as the Messiah of God. And when you find Me, you will be unselfish. When you find Me, you'll have no problem with your money. When you find Me, you will have found everything," because the Bible says we have come to fullness of life in Him. That's what Jesus was really saying to this young man.

He "looked at him and loved him." I like that because back in 1953 I was a very unhappy, confused young lad who was part of a broken home, alcohol, drugs, and violence. My life was so deeply scarred I wanted many times just to end it all. Then one day a group of kids I didn't know came by my house and invited me to some kind of a meeting at what they called a church. And I remember going to that meeting where the youth sponsor, God bless his heart, never went beyond the fourth grade and murdered the king's English when he taught. But he knelt down by my chair that night and said, "God loves you in spite of your confusion, in spite of the fact you don't know anything, in spite of the fact you haven't served Him or honored Him. God loves you with unconditional love." Something snapped in my life, and that night, as a seventeen-year-old kid, I walked down a church aisle and gave my heart to Christ. My life was never to be the same because it began with the fact that, no matter what I had done in my past, God loved me.

Brother, I don't care what you've done. I don't care about the stupid mistakes you've made in the past. I don't care how deeply you've marred and scarred your life with sin, or how dark the night of sin has been in your soul. I want you to know God loves you with an everlasting love. He proved that love in Jesus Christ.

There was a vacuum in that rich young ruler's life. He was within inches, literally, of having abundant life, of reaching fulfillment of what he was created for, but the Bible says he walked away. And you know what's interesting? Jesus let him go. I'm not sure we would today. I'm not so sure we wouldn't say, "Hey, just a minute. Come back here. I think we can work this thing out so everybody will be happy." No, Jesus let him go because the Lord brooks no rivals. He is Lord of all or not at all. Being a Christian is not just receiving Jesus Christ and the forgiveness of sins and the Holy Spirit. Those things are wonderful, and I praise God for them, but in return He gets us—lock, stock, and barrel. That's a man's Christianity. That's salvation.

You might be thinking, "There's something missing in my life. There's something not right in my life. The joy is not there. The thrill is not there. Something haunts me, like a gnawing emptiness that won't go away." No it's not a bad conscience. It's that Christ-shaped vacuum God has put in every man's life. And you can stuff all kinds of things in there. You can fill it with money, you can fill it with good times, you can fill it with booze, you can fill it with illicit sex. But it won't last. It won't satisfy until you fill it with Jesus Christ. That longing will continue to be there.

My story to you is that a seventeen-year-old Alabama boy

back in 1953 dared to open his heart's door and let Jesus Christ come in, and I have never regretted that one moment in my whole life. He's been my everything. "God so loved the world that He gave His only begotten Son, that whoever believes in Him should not perish but have everlasting life" (John 3:16, NKJV).

IT'S UP TO YOU

You're not reading this book by accident. You're reading it because the sovereign God brought it into your life. Perhaps there has been a gnawing in your soul, a pulling in your life, a wooing. Something is drawing you toward a new relationship with God. I want to tell you, that is the Holy Spirit. He has been after you to give you the wonderful news that God loves you unconditionally and He's willing to forgive you of every sin you've ever committed and to give you a new lease on life so you can start all over again. He's the God of the second chance, third chance, fourth chance, and fifth chance.

I believe there are three things God wants you to do. First of all, He wants you to do the hardest thing you will ever have to do. He wants you to acknowledge that you've sinned by simply saying, "Lord, I'm a sinner. I've broken Your Law. No matter how good I've tried to live, I haven't lived good enough because your Scripture says to 'be perfect…as your heavenly Father is perfect.' Lord, I'm a sinner." Let me tell you, it takes a man to say that. It takes guts and courage to say, "I have broken Your law. I have sinned." That's where the prodigal son started when he was in the pigsty. He said, "I have sinned. I will go to my father and say I have sinned."

Second, God wants you to confess faith in Jesus Christ. You say, "How do I do that?" The word *confess* means to "say the same thing." So say what Jesus says—that you believe He is the Son of God, that He is Messiah, that He is God's anointed, that He died on the cross, that He was buried in the grave, and that every demon in hell could not keep Him there. He rose, never to die again. He wants you to confess that.

Then He wants you to repent of your past sins. "How do I do that?" you ask. "Make it clear to me." The word *repent* means to "be sorry for one's sins"—sorry enough to turn and go in the opposite direction. That's what God wants you to do. In John chapter six, Jesus said to His disciples as people started to leave Him, "Do you also want to go away?" (John 6:67, NKJV). And the answer came back from the disciples, "Lord, to whom shall we go? You have the words of eternal life. Also we have come to believe and know that You are the Christ, the Son of the living God" (6:68–69, NKJV). Do you believe that?

If so, say to the Lord, "I want to start life all over again. This time in the will of God. This time under the blood of Jesus Christ. This time in repentance to my Savior." Do something that will affect your life for billions of years ahead, on into eternity. It's not a decision of time; it's a decision for eternity. Turn your life over to Christ.

A Chicago surgeon was awakened from his sleep at 2:30 in the morning on a blustery winter day. The nurse at the other end of the phone said, "Doctor, you must come. A little boy has been hit by a car, and he's bleeding profusely. He won't make it without your skilled surgical hand." The doctor put on his clothes and went out in the horrible subzero weather, driving several miles to the hospital. As he was stopped at a traffic light, waiting for the light to change, his car door suddenly opened, and a man wearing a brown coat and an old green hat pulled him out of the car, threw him on the ground, and drove his car away. As soon as the doctor recovered, he went to a phone booth to call the hospital. "A mugger has attacked me, and my car has been stolen, but I'll get there as quickly as I can," he said.

He hailed a cab, got to the hospital, walked to the emergency room, and was met with the words, "Doctor, what took you so long? The little boy just died. But would you come into the waiting room and comfort his parents?" As the doctor walked into the waiting room, he saw, in the corner, a man with a brown coat and an old green hat—the father of the boy who had died. That father had pushed away the one man who could have given life.

Don't push out of your life the One who can give you life: the Great Physician. Your marriage may depend on it. Your home may depend on it. The respect of your children may depend on it. And I'll tell you one thing that definitely depends on it—your eternity.

Don't wait another minute. Pray this prayer right now:

Lord Jesus, I believe You died for me on the cross. I confess I'm a sinner and cannot save myself. I invite You now to come into my life. I receive You now as my one and only Savior. Amen.

You may have been away from God for a long time. Maybe at one time in your life you made a profession of faith, and nothing came of it. Right now, turn your heart back over to God. Make that decision for Christ.

STUDY QUESTIONS

1. If someone were to write a "declaration" outlining your core beliefs, what would you insist be included?

2. Reread the story from Mark 10:17–22. What do Jesus' words in this story tell you about faith in God?

3. Which life stage best characterizes the way you *feel* about your faith in God: desperation, frustration, or salvation? Explain your answer.

4. Why do you suppose God allows us to feel desperate and/or frustrated in our faith and lives?

5. When are you tempted to look for meaning in life apart from your relationship with God?

6. How does Jesus give meaning to life?

7. What's one thing you discovered in this chapter that you'd like to share with someone else? When will you share it?

CHAPTER THREE

WALKING WITH GOD

JACK HAYFORD

I've long been impressed with a passage of Scripture that I believe speaks directly to men and their walk with the Lord. In Exodus chapter three, we read these words:

Now Moses was pasturing the flock of Jethro his father-in-law, the priest of Midian; and he led the flock to the west side of the wilderness, and came to Horeb, the mountain of God. And the angel of the LORD appeared to him in a blazing fire from the midst of a bush; and he looked, and behold, the bush was burning with fire, yet the bush was not consumed. So Moses said, "I must turn aside now, and see this marvelous sight, why the bush is not burned up." When the LORD saw that he turned aside to look, God called to him from the midst of the bush, and said, "Moses, Moses!" And he said, "Here I am." Then He said, "Do not come near here; remove your sandals from your feet, for the place on which you are standing is holy ground." He said also, "I am the God of your father, the God of Abraham, the God of Isaac, and the God of Jacob." Then Moses hid his face, for he was afraid to look at God. And the LORD said, "I have surely seen the affliction of My people who are in Egypt, and have given heed to their cry because of their taskmasters, for I am aware of their sufferings. So I have come down to deliver them from the power of the Egyptians, and to bring them up from that land to a good and spacious land…. And now, behold, the cry of the sons of Israel has come to Me; furthermore, I have seen the oppression with which the Egyptians are oppressing them. Therefore, come now, and I will send you to Pharaoh, so that you may bring My people, the sons of Israel, out of Egypt." But Moses said to God, "Who am I, that I should go to Pharaoh, and that I should bring the sons of Israel out of Egypt?" And He said, "Certainly I will be with you, and this shall be the sign to you that it is I who have sent you: when you have brought the people out of Egypt, you shall worship God at this mountain." (Exodus 3:1–12, NASB)

In that passage, the Spirit of God wants to reveal to us how life works in a relationship with the Father. Moses is a God-given picture of how a man can begin and continue a life of worship and prayer—a walk with God. The problem is that Moses seems so much larger than life that it's difficult to imagine ourselves in the same league. We've all seen Charlton Heston's portrayal of Moses, with his square jaw and four-foot-wide shoulders, and we have the idea we can't relate to Moses. But the fact is, you don't need to be built like Charlton Heston to be a man like Moses, and you don't have to be a religious expert to become a man of worship and prayer. If you will just look at this guy as a "plain duck" walking on the backside of the desert as we enter his life in this situation, you may see some of yourself in him.

I intentionally use the words "a plain duck walking on the backside of the desert" because a desert is not a great place for a duck. Moses' presence in this dry place has profound geographical significance, and what has happened in his life to bring him to the desert is even more profound. His life has application to us that is very practical and personal. I want you to note three elements in this passage to which God is calling us to respond: the *purpose*, the *place,* and the *path*.

THE FIRST PURPOSE OF WORSHIP:
DISCERN YOUR DESTINY

I believe every man says, "God, I would like to know You better. I would like to know how to go deeper with You. I would like to know how to go deeper into Your truth, deeper into Your wisdom, deeper into Your love, and deeper into Your power. Lord, I'd like to become a man of substance." Brother, the key to what's happening in the men's movement today is not its size. Don't make any mistake, it's thrilling to see God move in the lives of so many men. It's overwhelming. It's awesome. It's miraculous. But the secret to what's happening isn't the size. It's the substance. As we open up to the Lord and say, "Lord, I want to go deeper with You," there begins to settle into our souls what the Bible calls the weight of glory. And it's not a burdensome weight, like hefting something on your shoulder or dragging it by its heels. It's something substantial at the gut level of your being. I think every guy who is serious about the Lord wants it. His prayer is "God, I want to go deeper with You."

We need to settle why God calls us to be men of worship and prayer. It's not because He's interested in getting us to recite rituals, or take part in some form of programmed irrelevance, or behave in an unmanly way. Personal worship is a real obstacle for many Christian men. It's easy for us to function in a crowd of other Christians, but it's another thing to maintain a life of worship when we get back into our work or family environments. Even in the church we may fear that forthright worship of God will make us seem less manly. But the fact is, we're called to be men of worship and prayer all the time—even when we aren't surrounded by a gang of believers. How worship ever became stereotyped as unmanly is way outside my understanding. Worship is the most practical pursuit, and has the most powerful intent, of anything that will ever touch your life.

The text shows why that's true. God meets Moses, and something happens that reveals the purpose of worship in our lives. Worship is the way God has designed for us to *discern our destiny*. Worship is the way God has designed for me to learn what I'm about. I only find out who I am when I come to find out who He is, and I only come to know who He is when I get in His presence and spend time with Him. Moses had to spend time on holy ground and get in the presence of God to be called toward something greater than shepherding.

God is not calling us to wallow in a feeling of failure or an over-awestruck sense of amazement, though He certainly is worthy of praise. Instead, He says, "I want you to come and be with Me because, having created you, I'm the best possible source you have for finding out what I have in mind for you." You will find your destiny as you worship the Lord. He leads you. He directs you. If you want to know what God wants to do through your life, become a man of worship. In the eleventh verse of this chapter, Moses asks, "Lord, who am I?" And God answers his question in this setting of worship: "You are the one I've chosen."

THE SECOND PURPOSE OF WORSHIP: DELIVER YOUR FAMILY

The purpose of worship is not only to discern your destiny, but the second purpose is to *deliver your family*. God said to Moses, "I have called you here in My presence because a lot of people are in trouble, and you're related to them all." In Moses' case, his family involved a nation—a tribal group that included his brother and his sister, Aaron and Miriam, and an extended family of millions. But the issue was that it was *his* family. God calls a man to worship to deliver those people who are closest to Him. God was saying to Moses, "My heart aches because of what's happening to your family. I have asked you to come into My presence because what I do through you is going to change what is happening to them."

God calls men to worship not only to find out who they are

43

but to become instruments to help other people find freedom. And this point is pivotal to us in America who are watching a breakdown in families. Every Christian man represents a host of families, extended families, and communities. The Lord is saying to us, "I want to make a difference in families and towns. That's the way to make a difference in a nation." It's going to happen one man at a time, as we come to learn the purpose of God in saying, "Come be with Me." That is an important point: The purpose of a man's coming to worship and prayer is not to have some kind of mystical experience or to develop marvelous thoughts so he can sound like a guru. The purpose of worship is practical. You learn what you were made for, how to be better at it, and how to be an instrument of making other people free. God wants to make you such a man.

THE PLACE OF WORSHIP:
THE MOUNTAIN OF GOD

It's important to know *where* God will meet you to begin such a walk. There are two aspects of "place" in our text. The first is geography—what went on in the location itself. And the other is the encounter—what went on in the man. There was a place in Moses' life where he was ready to meet the Lord—not just a place on earth, but a place in his heart that was prepared.

Moses "came to Horeb, the mountain of God," which was the earlier name of what we call Mount Sinai. Horeb is a proper name, but it got the moniker "mountain of God" because a man came face to face with the Lord there. It gained a point of recognition, a point of designation, by reason of what happened there. I cannot help but think there is something really electric in this fact. The phrase "the mountain of God" not only occurs in the first verse, it bookends the passage. It's in both the opening verse and the last verse, verse one and verse twelve. At the front end it tells us this is where Moses met God. Then it says later, "This is where you're going to come learn to walk with Me and teach other people the same way." At the mountain of God, Moses grew in his walk with God and became mature as he spent time with God.

The mountain of God is referred to throughout Scripture. In the twelfth chapter of the Book of Hebrews we are told it is the same place that every person who worships today comes. When you and I worship, whether it be in the living room, in a car, in a stadium, or outside in the midst of God's creation, we come to the mountain of God. For Moses this was a *geographic* place, but for most of us that mountain is a *spiritual* place.

God has brought a lot of men to the mountain to have an encounter with Him so that when they go home, something will be renamed because of the walk they have begun with God. And just as Horeb's name was changed to Sinai, I believe there are pieces of real estate God wants us to retitle with His name because His presence comes there through godly men. Your home becomes a place that is designated differently because God is worshiped there. Your desk at work or your station in the factory becomes a "mountain of God" because you worship there, and people know that the man in this spot walks with God. Areas are impacted by the power of the Lord. Towns may not be renamed on the map, but they become different, spiritual places because they are where God touched a man. And because He touched a man, it made a difference in the world.

Brother, God wants you to come and have a daily walk with Him. He desires for you to establish a pattern of meeting Him, in which you come to be equipped and trained. There will be ongoing, permanent change as you meet with Him, a change that turns the most ordinary spot into the mountain of God.

THE PATHWAY OF WORSHIP: MOVING TOWARD MATURITY

What happened to Moses? God met him where he was. Moses was on the job, just doing his thing with the sheep and doing his best to make a living. He had been kicked out of Pharaoh's palace because of a rash act. He had left the royalty of Egypt for the reality of shepherding in the hills. Moses had grown up.

He didn't come, saying, "Lord I've earned these points, so now I'm qualified to become a great guy." The Lord met him where he was. Moses was a guy on the run. He wasn't a coward but a man under pressure. He hadn't been able to achieve his goals, to be what he was supposed to be. He tried to accomplish something on his own in Egypt and ended up being driven out of the area and running for his life because he experienced the same thing you and I do. At this point in his life, Moses might not have been a failure, but he was certainly a bit of a disappointment.

Have you ever felt that way? How many times have you said, "Lord, I believe I'm made to be somebody," but whenever you tried to do something great, it got fouled up and you ended up being less than you wanted to be? That's where the Lord met Moses. And that's where the revelation of the pathway came.

The path the Lord called Moses to was hard. Remember, he was out there in the desert and saw a glow on the mountainside, and the Bible says that Moses "turned aside." He turned from his shepherding to see what was going on with this fire. Most of you reading this book have already done that, you've already taken step one. Like Moses, you saw some supernatural evidence of God at work in this country, and you wanted to check it out. In taking that step, you're ready to see God work miracles in your own life. God sees that you've turned aside, and He's going to meet you.

And the Lord said, "Moses, Moses." The next step in the path toward God is to wait and listen for the voice of the Lord. Somewhere along that path you will hear God speaking to you. You will find how ready the Spirit of the Lord is to come and speak to your heart and tell you that He knows your name and that He has a plan with your name on it. What Moses experienced was hearing God's personal word to him: "You are My man, Moses. I know you."

God says, "I've written your name on the palms of My hand" (see Isaiah 49:16). God knows you. He wants you to walk with Him, spend time with Him, and become like Him. You were personally selected by God to have a personal *relationship* with Him. That's the revelation of God's Word. In the tenth chapter of the gospel of John, Jesus said, "I know every one of My sheep, and I call them by name." The Lord knows your name, and He's calling you to walk with Him.

The next thing the Lord said to Moses was "Take off your shoes." Why? First, because of what they represented. Along the way, Moses' shoes had picked up dust and dirt—things that are unworthy of God. The Lord wants us to come to Him clean—no sin unconfessed, no achievements paraded—just us, coming humbly before the Creator to worship Him.

The second reason God wanted Moses to take off his shoes was because they represented what he had fashioned with his own hands. When the Lord said, "Take off your shoes and stand there, on the ground," he was basically saying, "I want you to take off what *you've* made and to stand on what *I've* made." The Lord isn't impressed with our accomplishments. They only get in the way of His work. God is calling men today and saying, "I want you to strip down. First, to be rid of the evil that's been crammed into the cracks of your life for so long. Get rid of everything that smells of the past. Second, I want you in My presence to let *Me* do this. I want to show you how not to stand in your own power." God is in control of our walk, but we have to come before Him humbly, cleanly, and without pretense.

Psalm 46:10 says, "Be still, and know that I am God." It means to walk softly before the Lord—humbly. That's what God was saying to Moses, and it's the message He is sending to us today. As I move out of my own strut, dropping the self-confidence of my gait, I learn to wait on the Lord and move at His speed. The removal of shoes is a profound truth that speaks of our attitude in coming to God, trusting and relying on Him.

If you were to remove your shoes, you'd probably have a tough time getting through your day. When I wear shoes, I can move with all kinds of security and speed at any time, relatively free of the risk of stepping on something unpleasant. The fear of stubbing my toe or walking on the rocks doesn't even enter my mind, but when I take off my shoes, I walk a whole lot more carefully. That's why God calls me spiritually to "remove my shoes." He wants me to take the time to carefully consider what I'm doing with my time and my life. I tend to respond a lot more slowly to my wife. I respond more cautiously as I conduct business deals. And I'm a little bit slower to speak when I'm ticked off. A man who learns to walk with God and come into His presence daily takes off his shoes before the Lord. When he goes before the Father in worship, God says, "The place where you stand is holy, and I want you to come and stand in the territory I have made for you: holy ground." That's right: God created holy ground for you.

The holiest of all ground is where you stand to worship the Lord. And when you stand there, God begins to pour into your life His adequacy, His wisdom, His sufficiency, and His holiness so that walking with God in a life of worship and prayer and establishing a pattern of following His path opens a way into His presence.

It doesn't take long to get there. Begin your day by turning aside to be in the presence of the Lord. Having turned aside, I come to the place where I listen to His voice: "Lord, You have a plan for me today, for Jack, your servant." I start with a confession of what needs to be removed and the things I'm tempted to do in my own wisdom. Then I stand quiet before Him, to receive His counsel. That is the daily walk that I take to draw close to God. If you want to walk with God and to be filled with His holiness as you receive a fresh flow of His Spirit, follow that path. It leads into the presence of His Majesty.

STUDY QUESTIONS

1. If you could ask Moses one question about his encounter with God described in Exodus 3:1–12, what would you ask? How do you think he'd answer?

2. What makes you feel like worshiping God? How can we incorporate worship and prayer into our everyday lives?

3. Why do you think worship has power to change not only us but also those around us?

4. Where are the "spiritual places" in your life? How do you meet God there?

5. What part does pride play in worship and prayer? What part does humility play? What makes it difficult for you to be humble in your walk with God?

6. When was the last time you felt God's presence in your life? How do worship and prayer affect your ability to sense God's presence?

7. How would you like God to change your experience with worship and prayer? Ask God to begin that change this week.

CHAPTER FOUR

BEING A MAN
OF THE WORD

RAVI ZACHARIAS

My calling in life is that of a Christian apologist. The word *apologetics* comes from the Greek language, and it literally means to give an answer to the question of an antagonist. When you defend the Christian faith, you are involved in the task and the discipline of apologetics. A large amount of my time is devoted to defending the Word of God before antagonistic audiences, which has compelled me to become a student of God's Word.

Do you want to be a man of the Word? If you've already bent your knee to Him as Lord and Savior, you probably have a hunger for the Bible, for we know that "man shall not live by bread alone; but…by every word that proceeds from the mouth of the LORD" (Deuteronomy 8:3, NKJV). But perhaps if you are ruthlessly honest with yourself, the truth is you love God, but you are not a man of His Word. Maybe you are not yet convinced the Bible is absolute truth. Perhaps there is a barrier that keeps you from fully trusting it. You may be stuck behind the barrier of "discipline," or the barrier of "time," or even the barrier of "sin." But it's time to break through those barriers, and become a man of the Word.

Listen to what the apostle Paul said to Timothy, his son in the faith, in 2 Timothy 3:14–17: "But as for you, continue in what you have learned and have become convinced of, because you know those from whom you learned it, and how from infancy you have known the holy Scriptures, which are able to make you wise for salvation through faith in Christ Jesus." Then Paul adds the defining statement, "All Scripture is God-breathed and is useful for teaching, rebuking, correcting and training in righteousness, so that the man of God may be thoroughly equipped for every good work." In other words, *everything* you need as a man of God is provided in the Bible. The instructions God has given us, from rebuking to correcting to living a righteous life, can be found in Scripture.

Now the question is, do you merely believe the Bible to be some words from God, or are you unequivocally convinced that it is *the absolute revelation of God himself?* Paul said to Timothy, "You are convinced of the truthfulness of this." They were certain the Bible is true.

My prayer for you is the same certainty. I want you to come away from this chapter convinced that God has used His Word in history to transform nations. I also want you to remember that God has used His Word to transform individuals. His Word, dwelling in you, can empower you to resist all the allurements that stalk your life.

Two centuries ago, the skeptic Voltaire said, "In one hundred years, the Bible will be a forgotten book." Poor old Voltaire! He didn't know that after he died, one of his homes would belong to the French Bible Society and would be used as a warehouse for Bibles. God seems to have a sense of humor, allowing His Word to rise up and outlive its pallbearers.

NEAR TO THE TRUTH

As a young boy growing up in the city of New Delhi, I remember reading a story in my Hindi textbook called *The Treasure Is Nearer to You Than You Realize*. It's a beautiful little parable that offers an excellent point through a simple story. It tells of a wealthy man taking a long journey, and in his bag he had tucked away many of his precious stones and jewels. A thief began to follow him, pretending to be his friend but actually seeking a moment when he could be alone with the wealthy man's bags and steal those precious gems.

But the rich man, keenly aware of the designs of his companion, came up with a plan. Each night of his journey, he would stop at an inn, check into a room, and then suggest to the thief, "Why don't you wash up for the night? Here is a towel. After you come back, I'll go, and we can have a quiet night together here at the inn."

As soon as the thief would leave the room, the rich man would take all of his jewels and hide them. When the thief would return to the room, the rich man would go out to wash, leaving the thief to rummage around in the bags of the rich man. Although the thief searched everywhere, he never found anything of value.

At the end of that long journey, the rich man stepped aboard a train to go home, calling out to the thief as he did so, "I know why you've been following me. You've been trying to lay a hand on my treasure. You looked in my bags, you looked under my pillow, you looked in every corner of the room, but the one place you never looked was under your own pillow. If you had looked under your own pillow, you would have found all the treasure right there. Treasure was nearer to you than you realized!"

Brothers, treasure is nearer to us than we can ever imagine. As we hurry along, scurrying through life, looking for experiences and adventures that will enrich our lives, God is saying to us, "Here is the treasure. It's right with you, nearer than you ever dreamed." It's our Bible, and we neglect it at our peril.

THE VALUE OF SCRIPTURE

In Psalm 119, we are told of the value of Scripture. One hundred seventy-one of its 176 verses mention the Word of God directly. The psalmist sings out, "Your word is a lamp to my feet and a light to my path" (v. 105, NKJV). The Bible is a light—a lamp to guide us through the darkness. The psalmist also says, "Your word I have hidden in my heart, that I might not sin against You" (v. 11, NKJV). The Bible also has power—power to keep us from sin. What else in your life offers such resources? What else is so valuable?

In 2 Peter 1:19, the apostle Peter explains that "we have the word of the prophets made more certain, and you will do well to pay attention to it." In the context of that passage, Peter recounts one of the most glorious experiences of his life, an experience that was reserved for only two other disciples.

Jesus took Peter, James, and John to the top of a mountain, where the body of our Lord was transfigured. So brilliant was His glorified body that "His face shone like the sun, and his clothes became as white as the light." When Moses and Elijah also appeared from the heavens, Peter said to Jesus, "Why don't we build three tabernacles out here—one for you, one for Moses, and one for Elijah?" But the voice of God said, "This is my Son.... Listen to him!" At which the disciples fell flat on their faces, and their lives were dramatically transformed. (See Matthew 17:1–6.)

Peter experienced that marvelous episode firsthand, and in the light of that context he could later say, "But now we have a more sure word of prophecy." Do you see what he is saying? The life of Christ confirms all that was said by the prophets. Jesus is "the Word," and that Word is the ultimate confirmation of the truth. Peter was willing to take the Word as the ultimate evidence, beyond mere experience. Jesus Christ is the Word of God incarnate, and the Word gives wisdom. It gives power. It provides a measurement to tell me whether my life is right or wrong. We have the word of prophecy made more sure.

THE NATIONAL IMPACT OF SCRIPTURE

In the seventh century before Christ, an Old Testament king named Manasseh decided to do evil and lead his whole nation into idolatry. The king made three decisions. First, he decided to turn his back on the reformation of his father, Hezekiah. King

Hezekiah had ushered in one of the greatest spiritual revivals in Old Testament history, but when Manasseh came on the scene, the first thing he did was turn his back on those spiritual commitments. Second, he ushered in all kinds of heathen worship, turning the people away from God. Third, he began to persecute all of the prophets who were standing for the truth. In doing so, Manasseh readied the nation for destruction. When the Word was taken out, the country collapsed.

G. K. Chesterton, the famous theologian, philosopher, and journalist, once offered this bit of advice: "Whenever you remove any fence, always pause long enough to ask yourself the question, 'Why was it put there in the first place?'" You and I are living in the closing moments of the twentieth century, when fences are being removed all around us. America is playing a dangerous game with her destiny, removing fences that were put there for a reason. Fences that were put in place for our own spiritual protection. Fences for our national character. Fences for our families. Fences for the church of Jesus Christ. Fences that were built on the nature and character of God. And we are now trying to remove them.

Peggy Noonan, one-time speechwriter for President Reagan, noted in an article in the September 1992 issue of *Forbes* magazine:

> We have all had a moment when...we looked around and thought: "The world is changing, I am seeing it change." This is for me the moment when the new America began: I was at a graduation ceremony at a

public high school in New Jersey. It was 1971 or 1972. One by one a stream of black robed students walked across the stage and received their diplomas. And a pretty young girl with red hair, big under her graduation gown, walked up to receive hers. The auditorium stood and applauded. I looked at my sister. "She's going to have a baby."

The girl was eight months pregnant and had had the courage to go through with her pregnancy and take her finals and finish high school despite society's disapproval.

But: Society wasn't disapproving. It was applauding. Applause is a right and generous response for a young girl with grit and heart. And yet, in the sound of that applause I heard a wall falling, a thousand-year wall, a wall of sanctions that said: We as a society do not approve of teenaged unwed motherhood because it is not good for the child, not good for the mother, and not good for us.

The old America had a delicate sense of the difference between the general ("We disapprove") and the particular ("Let's go help her"). We had the moral self-confidence to sustain the...difference between "official" disapproval and "unofficial" succor. The old America would not have applauded the girl in the big graduation gown, but some of its individuals would have helped her not only materially but with some measure of emotional support. We don't do so much anymore. For all our tolerance and talk we don't show much love to what used to be called girls in trouble. As we've gotten more open-minded, we've gotten more closed hearted.

Then Peggy Noonan closes with these words: "Message to society: What you applaud, you encourage. And: Watch out what you celebrate."[1] We have to be wary of knocking down fences. Ideas that were abhorred, ideas that were once repulsive to us, ideas with which we were uneasy, we now celebrate. The fences have been removed. As one philosopher of ethics puts it:

> Ours is an age where ethics has become obsolete. It is superseded by science, deleted by psychology, dismissed as emotive by philosophy. It is drowned in compassion, evaporates into aesthetics, and retreats before relativism. The usual moral distinctions between good and bad are simply drowned in a maudlin emotion in which we feel more sympathy for the murderer than the murdered, for the adulterer than the betrayed, and in which we have actually begun to believe that the real guilty party, the one who somehow caused it all, is the victim and not the perpetrator of the crime.[2]

The fences have been removed in America, and that is exactly what happened in Israel seven centuries before Christ. All of a sudden there were idols in the valleys—idols where children were being offered into the burning arms of a god, where children's screams could be heard in the quietness of night, for child sacrifice had been instituted by Manasseh.

Retrace his steps for a moment. First, the king decided to turn his back on his father's spiritual commitments. Second, he began the worship of false idols. Third, he encouraged the persecution of those who stood up for the truth. It is possible for one human being who departs from the truth to lead millions into untold evil.

Some years ago I was in the home of Malcolm Muggeridge, possibly the greatest English journalist of the twentieth century. I had visited his home in Sussex, England, because his writings had a profound impact upon my life. As we were talking, he said something to me that stirred my imagination. He told me that Svetlana Stalin, the daughter of Joseph Stalin, had stayed in his home when the BBC was producing a film on the life of her father. "Three times," Mr. Muggeridge told me, "Svetlana talked of her father's death. Stalin was a small man, about five-foot-four and not very imposing, but a man of steel in terms of his personal ambition. His daughter said that just before he died, he sat up in his bed, clenched his fists towards the heavens, then threw his head back on the pillow and was gone. His daughter wanted to know if I could explain why he had done that."

For seventy years the nation of Russia lived under the cloud of atheism, their leaders shaking their fists in the face of God. They rejected the Word of God. Stalin himself obliterated fifteen million of his own people. And on his deathbed, the man who called himself "Steel" continued to fight against the truth.

Truly, one man, who rejects the truth, can lead millions into untold evil. The people of Russia still suffer today from their leader's rejection of God's Word.

THE INFLUENCE OF A CHANGED LIFE

When I was speaking at the Center for Geo-Political Strategy in Moscow, seven generals sat at my table. In the beginning they were very hostile, until I presented the gospel in the simple terms of what it can do in a man's life. Suddenly the tone of our meeting changed. People respond when they hear the truth, when they find out what the truth can do in a man's life.

As I was walking away from that meeting, past all the photographs of the great Russian generals hanging on the walls, the leading officer came up to me and clasped my hand. "Mr. Zacharias," he addressed me, "I believe what you have said to us about God is the truth…but it is so hard to change after seventy years of believing a lie."

One man was able to change the destiny of that nation. He rejected the truth, and the nation fell apart. You can go to Russia today and ask any leader to describe Russia's greatest problem, and he will tell you, "We are a nation skidding out of control. We have nothing to give our young people." The leaders of Russia were able to prepare freedom for the people, but they weren't able to prepare people for freedom, because the Word of God had not been given to them.

But now history is changing as Russians are turning to Christ by the thousands. If it's possible for one person to lead millions into evil, then it's just as possible for one man to bring truth to the nation.

Into such a setting came the man called Josiah. While Manasseh had led Israel into evil, Josiah decided to lead them out. Josiah became king not long after Manasseh died, and his first official act was to cleanse the house of God. He began literally to clean up the temple of God, washing the floors and putting the pieces back into place. And it was while they were cleaning the temple that they found the Word of God, which had been lost to a whole generation. Someone had hidden it in the floorboards (you can read all about it in 2 Kings 22). Josiah brought the Word of God into the palace, and tearing his clothes, he repented before God and bowed down and asked forgiveness for himself and his people.

Josiah gave the Word of God back to the people as he led the nation in national repentance, an act that rescued them from tyranny. The people began to live with the conviction of safety, but more importantly, it gave them the power to change. The nation was dramatically brought back to the true God, and a great revival was ushered in under the leadership of this twenty-year-old king. Josiah did one thing: He gave the Word of God back to the people.

Some time ago I had the privilege of being in San Juan, Puerto Rico, during a Billy Graham campaign. With us was Luis Palau, the great evangelist from Argentina and a coauthor of this book. He told me a story that caused my eyes to fill with tears.

Luis had just come from the solitary confinement cell of General Manuel Noriega, one-time strongman of Panama. The only things in that cell were an exercise bike, a cot, and a table with a Bible resting on it—a stark existence for a man who had once ruled his country. But all Noriega could talk about was his hunger for God and what God had done in his life while in solitary confinement. Before Luis left, the general told him that he no longer felt alone in that cell because he knew God was there with him. The Lord has transformed the life of a man who has done much evil.

Luis asked him, "If the day comes when you are released from prison, General, and you walk out a free man, what will you do with your life?"

General Manuel Noriega replied, "When I was president of Panama, I had three men in a tribunal who would come to me for counsel every morning. They would delineate all of the problems in the land, and then I would say to them, 'What do you think we should do?' They would invariably say, 'You are the commander in chief. We are here to tell you the problems, but we can't give you the answers. You must give them to us.' The commander is the one who knows what is best, and Mr. Palau, I have found a new general, a new commander in chief: Jesus Christ. When the day comes that I walk out of here, I am going to turn to my General and say, 'Lord, what do You want me to do?'" Then he pointed to his Bible and said, "There on that table is the book that tells me what His will is for my life. It has changed me."

God's Word has the power to change lives. Think about that the next time you are sitting at a big conference with thousands of other men. Every life has been changed by the power of God's Word. We can take comfort in the fact that His Word is truth, and it can change us whether we are worshiping with masses or sitting alone in a prison cell. Manuel Noriega has discovered how unfathomable is this treasure, how resourceful is the Word of God. It is a lamp for his feet, a light for his path, and greater than any experience he could have had. The Word of God instructs him as to the will of God. The same thing that happened in the lives of the Israelites under King Josiah can happen to you today. The Bible is still changing the lives of men.

THE PERSONAL IMPACT OF SCRIPTURE

The Lord Jesus once sat alone in the wilderness, about to start His ministry, when Satan came and tempted Him. "Why don't you turn these stones into bread?" the devil asked.

But Jesus said, "No, man shall not live by bread alone, but by every word that proceeds from the mouth of God." Had Jesus yielded to that temptation, he would have yielded to materialism.

Satan then changed his ploy. "Why don't You jump off the top of the steeple and see if Your Father will really send His angels to protect You, as it says in His Word?"

And Jesus replied, "It is also written, 'Do not put the Lord your God to the test.'" Jesus wasn't going to be tricked into the sin of doubting God. The devil wanted Jesus to be completely pragmatic, and not to exercise His faith. Had Jesus yielded to the sin of pragmatism, there would have been no cross of salvation. Pragmatism which only serves the moment is destructive in the long run.

So Satan came right back with a third temptation, showing Jesus all the treasures in the world and suggesting, "All this I will give you, if you will bow down and worship me."

This time Jesus came back sharply: "Be gone, Satan! For it is written, 'You shall worship the Lord your God, and Him only shall you serve.'" Had Jesus given in, He would have been guilty of hedonism—the sin of pleasure alone as life's ultimate purpose.

Do those temptations sound familiar? Materialism—do only that which is good for matter. Pragmatism—do whatever seems best in the short term. Hedonism—do what feels good. Jesus rejected all three of them with Scripture, instead reminding us, "You shall worship the Lord your God alone, and Him only shall you serve." (See Matthew 4:1–11.)

I draw two simple conclusions from this. Whether it is for the history of a nation, or an individual in temptation, the Word of God is what makes the difference. Jesus quotes the Book of Deuteronomy to Satan and is able to triumph over temptation.

How can God change history? By His Word.

How can God change your life and equip you to fight temptation? By His Word.

I have three children. When they were little, I would tell them fairy tales, and they would get all excited as I'd talk about dragons and fighting men with swords. But as they grew older, my stories had to change to maintain their attention. The older you get, the more it takes to fill your heart with wonder. Only God is big enough to fill the heart of a grown man. The difference between a fairy tale and the Word of God is that the fairy tale is merely fantastic, while the Word of God is fantastically true.

At every coronation of a monarch of England, the Bible is

presented to the new monarch, and these words are said: "This Book is the most valuable thing the world affords." What's true of kings is equally true of the sons of the King of kings. Your Bible is your most valuable asset. It can truly change your life.

During Christmas of 1939 King George VI delivered a speech. Years later those words would come back to serve him when he was dying of cancer: "I said to the man at the gate of the year, 'Give me a light that I may walk safely into the unknown.' And he said to me, 'Go out into the darkness, and put your hand into the hand of God, and it shall be to you better than the light and safer than the known.'" Put your hand into the hand of God, and He shall guide you. His Word shall be a lamp for your feet and a light for your path.

Christian, I don't know a better way to put your hand into the hand of God than to take Him at His Word and be obedient to it. In His Word there is power for national destiny—and power for individual purity. When you hide His Word in your heart, you become a man of integrity. "Your word I have hidden in my heart, that I might not sin against You."

[1] Peggy Noonan, "You'd cry too if it happened to you," *Forbes,* 14 September 1992, 69.

[2] Robert E. Fitch, "The Obsolescence of Ethics," *Christianity and Crisis: A Journal of Opinion* 19 (16 November 1959): 163–65.

STUDY QUESTIONS

1. What "barriers" keep you from spending time in the Bible?

2. Finish this sentence: "The Bible is like a valuable treasure because..."

3. Read the original story of Josiah in 2 Kings 22–23. Why do you suppose simply reading and hearing the Scripture had such an impact on so many people?

4. How have you seen the Bible transform people's lives today?

5. Describe how your life might be different if you couldn't read the Bible.

6. What verse of Scripture has been especially meaningful to you in the past? Why was it so meaningful?

7. What can you do this week to help someone else grow in his commitment to be a man of God's Word?

CHAPTER FIVE

HONORING OTHERS

GARY SMALLEY

T here is a word which all men ought to hold dear. Just one simple word, yet it is the most powerful word I know. After thirty years of ministering around the world, I believe this word has become the most important word in my life, a word that has literally changed my life. It's changed my marriage. It's at the heart of all healthy relationships, marriages, and families. If we're going to be men of integrity, this word needs to be on our hearts. Some men, after studying this word, will never be the same. The word will become a major part of their lives.

The word is *honor*. It is the number-one need of your wife, of your kids, of your friends, and of your pastor. It's the number-one need of your coworkers and your friends. It's the key to a successful business. As I've observed the power of honor in my life and my relationship with Christ, I've come to realize I cannot have the kind of relationships that God wills for me without an understanding of honor.

INCREASING YOUR HONOR

Honor is the basis of all things God created that are admirable and praiseworthy. In fact, the word literally means "attaching high value to someone or something." If you've ever been to a banquet and stood to applaud when a person of great significance came into the room, you have demonstrated honor. Any time you are in the presence of people you consider great, you treat them with honor. You defer to them. You tell them what a privilege it is to meet them. You might even bow slightly. What you are saying by bowing is that you highly esteem them.

If you've ever been surprised to meet someone special, you might have dropped your jaw or had a special light come into your eyes that said, "Wow, I'm honored to meet you." When you are with someone you honor, you take special notice. In some cultures, you are even expected to kneel.

Years ago, John Trent and I wrote a book called *The Blessing*. The Hebrew word translated "blessing" means to bend your knee in the presence of someone very valuable. That's why the Scripture says, "Come, let us bow down in worship, let us kneel before the LORD our Maker; for he is our God" (Psalm 95:6–7), and "Bless the LORD, O my soul; and all that is within me, bless His holy name" (Psalm 103:1, NASB). When we bless the Lord, we're signifying that we honor God above everything in creation. We're saying, in effect, "God, You are most important to me. You are greater than I. I kneel in your presence."

The Lord Jesus once said that where our treasures are, that's where our hearts are also. You know, I treasure the Lord. I treasure my relationship with Him. I start every day by honoring Him. The first thing I say each morning is "Father, nothing else on this earth means more to me than You. You are my life. You are the living well within me that springs up and brings me life in never-ending wealth." Years ago my life changed when I realized that nothing is more important on this earth than my relationship with Christ. He is my life. Everything else is overflow. I can enjoy failure or success because I always know that the essence of my life is my relationship with Christ. He is the one I bow to; He is the one I honor above all others. Whomever or whatever we honor, that's where our heart is.

Do the people in your life feel honored? You may not feel like honoring your bride today, but in the Bible, God calls you to honor her. Ephesians chapter five says that you ought to treat her the same way Christ treats His church—with honor. Even if you don't feel like it.

If you increase the honor you give your wife every day, and if you show her she is extremely important to you, within a very short time your feelings will catch up to your decision. If you'll treat your children with honor, as though they were highly valued and respected, you'll find yourselves in a new and wonderful relationship. Learn to honor your boss and your coworkers, and you'll find refreshment and blessing from the Lord. I've even come to the place where I can honor the trials in my life because the storms that come into my life are part of God's design to make me like His Son. So I've learned to honor them. I want to honor everyone, friends and foes alike, for God loves each one so much He was willing to die for them. I give the Lord thanks for all things, for this is the will of Christ Jesus. I can look forward to the future, knowing that everything that happens to me calls for a response of honor.

THE CHILDREN OF THE KING

To help you remember this concept, consider the people you sit next to at church. The people beside you, in front of you, and behind you are royalty. They are all children of the King! Can you get any more significant than a child of the King? They are here as God's ambassadors, representing Him to the world. Just think of that for a moment. If you know the Lord, you are a child of the King. That makes you royalty.

Imagine the response you'll get from people if you begin treating them like royalty. What would happen if you walked up to your pastor next Sunday, got on your knees, and said, "I can't believe I worship at the same place where you preach." He wouldn't know how to handle it!

When we were raising our three kids, we did it like most people do: trial and error, trying to learn to be the best parents possible. I didn't have an example from my parents of how to love kids, so I had to learn it on the job. When I learned about the concept of honor, we created a family constitution. The fifth article of our constitution speaks of honoring God and His creation—all people and all things. My son, Michael, would be watching TV, and I'd walk into the living room and get down on my knees and say, "Michael, I can't believe I'm in the same home with you. This is incredible!" You know what he would say? "Dad, you are so strange." But did he appreciate it? Yes, because he knew he was honored. It's incredible how many stories I've heard from Promise Keepers who went home and knelt before their wives and prayed a prayer of thanks, or gave them applause. It's amazing how it affects them. They feel cherished. They feel special. One of our deepest needs as humans is to feel respected. When you honor people, you remind them of how special they are before God.

I used to ask my boys, "What is the greatest thing in life?" And they would answer, "Honoring God and people." We said it all the time since it was part of our family constitution. I wanted to make sure they grew up understanding the concept of honor. Nothing can make more difference in their relationships than the practice of that word.

HONORING YOUR WIFE

It is my dream to help thousands of men all over the world develop a new sense of honor for their wives. I want them to think about how to increase the value of their wives. One way to do that is to help men see the uniqueness of their brides. Your wife is unique. She isn't like anyone else, and she is perfect for you. Every cell in her body is different from your cells. That's the way God created her. And her uniqueness is extremely important to your life, your friendships, and your relationship with God.

When I first got married, I didn't really know how to honor my wife; I didn't understand the concept. I didn't know how to love her as Christ loved the church. I had to learn that God considers us so valuable He sent His only begotten Son that we might have eternal life. He loves us so much He was willing to sacrifice. He honored us by putting us first, even though we didn't deserve it. And that's how He was calling me to love my wife.

Five years into my marriage the relationship was going

downhill rapidly. I wanted to go to a counselor, but she didn't have any hope that I could figure things out. I came home from my church one day and asked my wife for the thousandth time, "What's wrong with our marriage? Why can't we get this together?" And my wife said to me, "I feel like everything on this earth means more to you than I do."

I just stood there, staring. Then I asked her to help me understand. She said the television set meant more to me than she did because I would come home and go right to the TV, as though she didn't even exist. Now all of us would agree that our televisions are not more important than our wives, but without even realizing it, many times we imply that by our actions. It had never occurred to me that my TV watching had that effect on her. In addition, I had put my work above my relationship with her. I had put my golf game above my commitment to her. I had made fishing more important than building up my wife.

First Peter 3:7 reads, "Husbands..., live with your wives in an understanding way" (NASB). Recognize she's a woman, very sensitive and alert, and different from you. I hadn't lived with her in understanding, so I needed to change. "Grant her honor as a fellow heir of the grace of life, so that your prayers may not be hindered," Peter continues. I had not honored her, and my prayers and spiritual life were hindered because I had failed to do so.

So that very day I got down on my knees in front of my wife, and I told her, "I treasure you above all other human beings, above all other things on this earth, above the television, above fishing, above golf, and above my work." I confessed my sin that I had not treasured my wife as God wanted me to. And I said to her in our little kitchen in our first home, "From this day on I purpose, I promise, that nothing on this earth will keep me from honoring you. My relationship with Christ is the most important thing to me, since He's the one I worship, but above everything else on this earth, you're number one."

As soon as I said it, my heart sank. I felt sick to my stomach. I thought she would take advantage of me. I feared I'd be home all the time, talking and going shopping with her and doing all kinds of things that women love and men can't stand. But you know what happened? When she felt like a queen in my life, she relaxed and began to push me into the things she knew I enjoyed. I used to have to say that I would rather be with her. And she would make me do things I liked to do. Because when a woman feels secure that she has first place in your life, she'll relax. That is one of her deepest needs, to feel the security and honor that a man loves her with all of his heart.

I didn't know how to do that because I wasn't raised in a home where that was modeled. I never once saw my dad hug my mom. I was raised with arguments and accusations. My dad never knew how to honor his wife because his dad didn't know how. I don't blame any of my ancestors; I forgive them. But when my kids were younger, we sat them down, and I told them how my dad and my grandfather had goofed up. And my kids said to me, "Yes, dad, that's one of the reasons you're so goofed up." Then we decided to pray for forgiveness for my father and grandfather and start a whole new generation as a family. It's not too late to start a new legacy of honor in *your* marriage as well.

REVEALING HONOR

If your wife is royalty, she's like a celebrity. I once asked my wife to autograph an 8" x10" picture of herself and put it in my office so that every day I would be reminded I live with royalty.

The first thing I do every morning is look at her, take a deep breath, and say, "Unbelievable! I'm actually lying right next to the most important person on this earth." It makes me want to jump out of bed and cheer! That sort of attitude changes your heart, men. It's a gift we give, this gift of honor. Your wife may ask you what's wrong and feel your forehead initially, but she'll begin to appreciate the fact that you honor her above all others.

This probably won't come naturally to you because it requires you to approach your wife on her turf. Research shows that as soon as boys are born, their arms and legs are moving significantly more than girls are. We're active, and as we grow up, we want activity. Guess what is moving on that little girl right up to birth? Her lip muscles. Really! She's getting herself ready to communicate. I believe one of the reasons women outlive us by about ten years is because they are better communicators. Doctors say you are healthier when you learn how to communicate intimately with others. Some insurance companies put out brochures targeting men and asking them to please learn how to communicate with their wives so they'll live longer. So learn to communicate. Reveal your honor by taking the time to communicate.

Men have a tendency to be competitive. We want to win; that's part of our nature. We find friendship and camaraderie in doing activities together. But the average woman doesn't want to compete; she wants to cooperate. Your wife wants to connect with you, and she'll do it with words. Intimacy to a woman is words spoken by two people who understand and honor each other. Intimacy to a man is doing something together. We don't have to say a word. For the average male, wrestling with his wife is more intimate than talking with her. Going someplace with her or taking a walk is how we communicate.

So learn to communicate on her level. Make an effort to put your feelings into words. The Bible says that God created woman to be our completer. Remember, it's not good for man to be alone. Your wife gives you something you can't have on your own. She offers the relational connection to your life that not only helps you live longer, but completes your life.

God has given your wife a natural desire to have a great relationship with you, and a natural ability to recognize a great relationship. Right in your home is a built-in marriage manual. You can literally ask her where you are on a scale of zero to ten in your marriage, and she'll know. Every woman knows. So develop the habit of confessing your maleness to your wife by saying, "I don't mean to be like this a lot of times; I know it's offending you. But I'd love to ask you to forgive me." When you ask forgiveness from your wife, you reveal your honor and drain her of anger. As the anger drains, she can become the completer God designed her to be.

It will sometimes be a struggle. Take shopping. Go to a mall with your wife, and what's the first thing you want to know? "Why are we here?" She'll say she's there to buy a coat. So you move along toward the coat store. She tries on this coat and that coat, but she doesn't actually buy a coat. It starts to frustrate you. She goes to the next store and tries on more coats. It frustrates you more. Why? Because we are not shopping for coats, we are *hunting* for coats. We want to shoot the coat, bag it, and get out of there. What are they doing? They are connecting to everything. On the way to the coats, they touch stuff. We don't want to touch anything. They're touching all this stuff because they're connecting with everything. Going to the mall for a woman is a life experience. For the average man, it's a headache. But it's a great way of revealing our honor to our wives.

HONORING OTHERS

I used to think you had to like people to honor them. I thought they had to be performing well before you could honor them. But honor has nothing to do with performance. It has everything to do with attitude. Honor is a gift of grace. It shows the other person that you value him or her. Honor is something you give a person without his having to earn it.

Did we earn the love of God? No. Did Christ come to die in your place because you did something worthwhile? No. While we were yet sinners, Christ died for us. We were shaking our fists in God's face, saying we didn't want Him, yet He sent His Son to die for us because He valued us dearly. What an honor. Now you, in response to God's honoring you, can do the exact same thing for others. You can honor your wife. Show her you love her by sacrificing what you want for what she wants. You can honor your children. Say something supportive, even when they haven't "earned" it. You can honor your employer. Do your best work without complaint, and let him or her know you appreciate the opportunity to serve in your position.

The very first command with a promise in all the Bible is to honor your mother and father so "that it may go well with you" (Ephesians 6:2–3). When was the last time you honored your father? Reveal your respect for him. Tell him you love him. Honor your mother by expressing your appreciation of everything she went through in raising you. When you honor them, things will go well with you.

Even if you were raised in an abusive situation, God gives the grace to honor trials. We can literally honor a mother and father who abused us by making a decision to show them respect. It is your decision to value them. They don't have to earn it. I can almost guarantee you that they were abusive because they were abused as kids. Chances are, if you were abused, your grandfather abused your parent. The Bible says that the sins of the fathers are visited onto their children to the third and fourth generation (Exodus 34:7), so you could be suffering today because of a great-great-grandfather and blaming your parents for it instead of loving them and giving them honor, which is God's will for our lives. It's tough to develop peace in your life and to have a sense of honor if you've never forgiven your parents for their mistakes and made a decision to honor them.

You can take control of your life by starting to honor others. You can strengthen your marriage by honoring your wife. You can develop close friendships by choosing to honor other men. One of the keys to spiritual growth is getting together with other men on a weekly basis in a small group to hold one another account-able. You'll find great strength in having others support you in your walk with God.

If you want to strengthen your relationships, decide to honor others. And if you want to strengthen your walk with God, make a decision in your heart to honor Him above all others. As you do, you'll find that honor starts to change your life, just as it did mine.

STUDY QUESTIONS

1. How has honor been demonstrated to you in the past?

2. In practical, everyday language, what does it mean to give honor to God?

3. In what ways does your attitude toward others change when you consider them as children of the King? How does that affect your actions?

4. Describe the last time you treated your wife like royalty. Now describe what the next time will be like.

5. How is it possible to honor someone without liking him or her?

6. Why do you suppose God commands us to honor our parents?

7. What rewards might come from giving honor to our children? What's one thing you can do this week to honor your kids?

CHAPTER SIX

KEEPING COVENANTS

DENNIS RAINEY

W hat is taking place in the American family today reminds me of the Ed Sullivan show in the 1950s. Perhaps you recall the German performer Eric Brenn, who would come out with some long sticks and a handful of plates. He would put a plate on a stick and begin to spin it, and after he got the first plate spinning, he would move to a second plate, a third plate, a fourth plate, a fifth plate, and so forth until he had about eight plates spinning.

And I can recall, as a little boy in southwest Missouri, watching what was happening with that first plate on the end. It would begin to wobble. Then suddenly, as though he could hear me yell at him all the way from my hometown to Ed Sullivan's studio, Brenn would rush back and spin that first plate again. And on he would go, with the ninth, the tenth, the eleventh plate—running back and forth through the entire act, until he eventually had fifteen to eighteen plates spinning. Then, just when you thought he couldn't keep them going any longer, he would start at one end of the table and gather them up as if he were going to the cupboard. How could anybody keep so many things juggling at once?

Today, two people decide to become one. We leave, we cleave, and we become one flesh. As newlyweds, we're excited about this relationship called marriage. We spin the plate and give it our very best shot. We nurture it, we cherish it, and we keep it spinning. Then things begin to happen. Job responsibilities increase. We get transferred to another location, perhaps away from our extended family. There are civic responsibilities, and this plate called marriage, which once got all our attention, now gets only the leftovers—an occasional "maintenance spin." And then something happens that really impacts this plate called marriage: We get some little saucers.

I have six of these saucers, and I want to tell you, you *can* spin them, but they take a lot of energy. You get a few of these little saucers spinning, and pretty soon the marriage relationship doesn't even get a maintenance spin. Then something happens to one of these saucers; it turns into a platter. Now you've got real problems. One day the platter is oblong, the next day it's square. One day it looks like a saucer again, and the next it's back to being a platter. Now it's pretty tough to spin. It's a teenager!

The effect on the marriage plate is significant, and a lot of relationships wobble so much they fall to the floor and shatter. And when a marriage relationship shatters, it isn't just a marriage that breaks up, but a family. When a large number of families break up, the country itself begins to be damaged. Two other plates are impacted as well when the marriage plate falls to the ground: the antique plates. Both sets of parents have been dishonored.

REMEMBER YOUR VOWS

Today there is a great need in our country to come back to this plate called marriage and to address the commitment we have made. We've spent the better part of three decades watching unprecedented social experimentation on marriages and families, and it's time we stop ignoring God and come back to His blueprint for marriage.

Psalm 127:1 says, "Unless the LORD builds the house, they labor in vain who build it" (NKJV). Certainly, a lot of vain building is going on today. We see a generation of children confused, insecure, shaken, and bewildered by broken promises.

A young lad returned home from school one afternoon crying. His mom and dad came to him, put their arms around him, and said, "What's wrong, son?"

The boy was sobbing uncontrollably, but finally he gathered himself and said, "I want two mommies and two daddies!"

His mother and father looked at each other. "What do you mean you want two mommies and two daddies?"

"Everybody in my class has two mommies and two daddies," he said, "and I'm the only one who has only one mom and dad."

This shouldn't be! This is not what God called us to do and to be as covenant keepers. Let me ask you some questions as you consider the damage being done. What makes a child four times more likely to commit a violent crime? What increases the likelihood of a child's living in poverty, dropping out of school, and becoming a juvenile delinquent? What increases the chances of a child's abusing alcohol, taking drugs, becoming sexually promiscuous, or committing suicide? What contributes one million children each year to the millions who have already been damaged? Divorce. And it is killing America.

In Malachi 2:16, God doesn't hedge His words when He states, "I hate divorce." Divorce tears apart children, families, and even nations. And I believe we are on the precipice of either a great spiritual awakening or anarchy. I am convinced that the key commitment you and I must make in our homes is this relationship called marriage. Marriage is not some kind of social contract. It's not an experiment that is to be littered with prenuptial agreements. Nor is it simply a convenience based upon what's good for *me*. Marriage is a covenant, a sacred vow between one man and one woman and their God, for a lifetime.

Do you remember your vows? I said, "In the name of God, I, Dennis, take you, Barbara, to be my wife. To have and to hold from this day forward, for better and for worse, for richer and for poorer, in sickness and in health, to love and to cherish until parted by death. This is my solemn vow." I vowed to cherish, honor, esteem, value, and give up my life for Barbara. But today far too many Christian men are not having and holding. They are letting go. We need to return to a tenacious commitment to our partner in marriage.

Winston Churchill, when called a "bulldog" for being too obstinate, said, "The nose of a bulldog is slanted backward so that he can continue to breathe without letting go." We need more Christian men who will not let go. We need men who are willing to stand up for their vows and their covenants and make their marriages work. Let's look at three marks of a covenant keeper.

FEAR THE LORD

The first mark of a covenant keeper is that he fears God. One of the reasons I believe we break our vows so easily today is that we no longer fear God's judgment and wrath. We no longer live with the fear of displeasing Him. Instead, we have been caught up in a culture that encourages us to feed our narcissistic desires.

Proverbs 8:13 tells us, "The fear of the LORD is to hate evil; pride and arrogance...I hate" (NKJV). One of the major reasons Christian marriages are falling apart is because of proud, arrogant Christian men. We are selfish. And until we return to the biblical viewpoint of who we are—selfish, depraved creatures in need of the Savior—then we've had it. It has been said that a superficial view of God will give birth to a shallow view of sin. And certainly those who do not learn the fear of the Lord will find themselves caught in sin.

The definition of "the fear of God" is to hold Him in awe and respect. Yes, He is a God of love, but He is also a God of justice, a God of wrath, and a God who must punish sin. That's why He sent His Son. When we practice the presence of God and live our lives recognizing that He looks down from heaven, watching every choice we make, we are practicing the fear of God.

I'm a product of the Jesus Movement. My spiritual roots go back to a time when people talked about the love of God. It's what brought me to Him. But what we need today in our churches and in our own lives is a fresh return to the fear of God—a reminder that He is a God of justice, wrath, and anger. The fear of the Lord helps me, as a man, to keep my covenant.

A number of years ago I was in a meeting in Minneapolis. At the end of the morning session, I opened the stairway door to go outside, and there on the floor in front me was a pornographic magazine, laid open to the centerfold. I'm amazed how many thoughts can go through a mind instantaneously. My first thought was "No one would know." Then instantly, "God would know." Then other thoughts: "I'll have to tell Barbara. I'll have to tell my kids. I'll have to confess to my church." And so, in a split second, I stepped over what I believe was a major trap in my life.

Proverbs calls sin a snare. And I want to tell you, I stepped over a snare, a trap. At the end of that day, after I had completely forgotten about the trap at the top of the stairs, guess what was still there? The same magazine. I could have picked it up and taken it to my room. There was still no one there. Except One. Practicing the presence of God was what turned me away from sin.

When you channel surfed the last time you were in a hotel room, did you stop on the wrong channel? I'll tell you what keeps me from stopping: knowing that my holy, heavenly Father Who went to a cross and died for me, Who loved me enough to chase me down when I was a young rebel, sees every act I commit. And His love for me, along with my fear of Him, motivates me to obey Him and turn away from evil.

Someone has said sin would have fewer takers if its consequences occurred immediately. A covenant keeper lives as though those consequences are immediate.

We need today something similar to what occurred in the fifteenth century. At that time there was a group of men called the Reformers. Their rally cry: *Coram Deo*, which means "before the eyes of God." Today we need a Family Reformation, led by men who are willing to cry, "*Coram Deo!*" and then live their lives with a healthy fear of God.

LOVE YOUR WIFE

Not only does a covenant keeper fear God, but he vows to love his wife like the Savior. Remember, Ephesians 5 tells us to love our wives by giving ourselves up for them. We ought to love our wives as our own bodies. "He who loves his own wife loves himself; for no one ever hated his own flesh, but nourishes and cherishes it" (vv. 28–29, NASB). You and I are called to be lovers of our wives. This begins by telling our wives very simply, "I love you."

I recently had the privilege of going to an executive's birthday party in Miami, Florida. The man was eighty years old, and he and his wife were celebrating fifty-five years together as a couple. His words marked him as a covenant keeper, as one who recognizes the need to love and care for his wife. He had written the following: "We've been married fifty-five years, and we still tell each other 'I love you' all the time. We say it the first thing every morning, and it's the last thing we say to each other before we go to sleep." He went on to write, "My only regret is that my wife is most likely to outlive me. I won't always be around to take care of her. I know the Lord will do it, but in the meantime I am glad he uses me."

As I publicly repeated the words of this octogenarian at his party, he began to weep. But I wish you could have seen the look in his wife's eyes—she began to beam. He had told his wife he loved her in a simple, yet profound way.

Another way we can love our wives like the Savior is to pray together. Lead her spiritually. Twenty-five years ago I asked an older mentor of mine, "What's the best advice you'd give me as a newlywed?" He put his arm around me and said, "I would encourage you to pray with your wife every day. No matter what. Pray with her."

And so, being a young, newly married man, I decided to do just that, and it has been the best spiritual discipline in our marriage relationship. Sometimes when we go to bed, my wife faces one wall and I face the other. It is symbolic of something between us. And the Lord will come to me in my conscience and say, "Hey, Rainey, are you gonna pray with her?" And I reply, "No, Lord, I don't like her tonight." And He says, "Well, you are the one who tells them at those conferences that you pray with your wife!"

Of course, I normally respond with "That's a cheap shot, Lord." And the conversation will go on until finally I roll over and pray with her. I don't like admitting fault; I don't like admitting my responsibility for failing her. The fact is, sometimes she is more at fault. But I'm the leader of this family, and I'm the one who has to take responsibility for the marriage. I am convinced that we remain married because of that simple discipline of praying with one another. It keeps us connected to our God and to each other every day.

BE A SERVANT

A third mark of a man who keeps his covenant is that he leads like a servant. Mark 10:35–45 tells us what Jesus Christ said was the way to greatness. "The Son of Man did not come to be served, but to serve, and to give His life a ransom for many" (v. 45, NASB). And He tells us men, as the leaders of our homes, that if we want to lead our families, we must serve. One of the reasons feminists are so angry today is that we have not served women with selfless love. We are guilty of using women. We are guilty of abusing them. But the Bible is the hope for men to give up their rights, to give up their egos, to give up their arrogance, and to empty themselves and become lovers like Christ. It tells us to lead our wives as Christ led the church.

We have heard far too much about rights in our culture. I am sick of rights. We now have fifty states with "no fault" divorce. What's no one's fault is no one's responsibility. It's time to stop talking about our rights and start talking about what God demands of us as leaders.

Bill Bright, the president and founder of Campus Crusade for Christ, gave me a piece of advice I'll never forget. He told me that early in their marriage both he and his wife, Vonette, did something unusual. They wrote a contract and signed over to the Lord the title deed to their lives. That piece of paper formally proclaimed that Jesus Christ was the sole owner and Lord of their lives.

I was mighty impressed with that thought, so on Christmas Day 1972, before we gave each other any gifts, Barbara and I went into separate rooms, took out sheets of paper, and did the same thing. We gave up all of our rights, all of our expectations, all of our dreams, and all of our hopes. We just gave them all to God. It was Barbara's and my way of saying, "God, we are yours. We are bond servants, and we want you to know we're going to formalize this by signing and dating this deed." The most valuable documents in our safe-deposit box are the two sheets of paper that settled the issue of who would be Lord and Master of a young married couple's life together.

A man who leads like a servant also cares for his wife's needs. Do you know what her top three needs are right now? Maybe she needs a romantic date. Maybe she needs a sense of security. Ask her the question, "Honey, what are your top three needs right now? What is your greatest fear, your greatest worry? What's your most profound dream? What new vista would you like to have in the next twenty years together as a couple?"

Willard Harley interviewed over twenty-two hundred women and listed their top five needs. The fifth greatest need of a woman was family commitment. Number four was financial support. Number three was honesty and openness with her husband. Number two was conversation. And the greatest need of a woman—and this may surprise you—was affection. Women want nonsexual affection: tender words, letters, a gentle touch, affection that is given without any demand to meet our needs as men. A servant leader asks God to help him learn to fulfill his wife's needs.

I once saw a report by an eleven-year-old boy, describing his home. He said, "My mother keeps a cookie jar and we can help ourselves, except we can't if it is too close to mealtime. Only Dad can anytime. When he comes from the office, he helps himself no matter if it is just before we eat. He always slaps my mother on the behind and brags about how great she is and how great she can cook. Then she turns around and they hug. The way they do it, you'd think they just got married or something."

Now, listen to what the boy says as he concludes: "It makes me feel good. This is what I like best about my family."

One of the best illustrations of what a covenant keeper looks like was shared with me by Crawford Loritts. For twenty-two years Robertson McQuilkin served faithfully as the president of Columbia Bible College and Seminary in Columbia, South Carolina. When his wife of over forty years was diagnosed as having Alzheimer's disease, he was forced to make the decision of staying in his post as president or going home and being with his wife, Muriel. Here's what he said at chapel before the students and faculty:

> My dear wife, Muriel, has been in failing health for about eight years, and so far, I have been able to carry both her growing needs and my leadership responsibilities here at the school. But recently it has become apparent that Muriel is contented most of the time she is with me and none of the time when I'm away from her. It is not that she is just discontent. She is filled with terror, fear that

she has lost me. She goes in search of me when I leave home. Then she may be full of anger when she cannot get to me. So it is clear to me that she needs me now full-time. The decision was made to stay with her, in a way, forty-two years ago, when I promised to care for Muriel in sickness and in health, 'til death do us part.... As a man of my word, integrity has something to do with it. But so does fairness. She has cared for me fully and sacrificially as my wife all these years. If I cared for her for the next forty years, I would not be out of debt. Duty, however, can be grim and stoic. But there is more. I love Muriel. She is a delight to me—her childlike dependence and confidence in me, her warm love, an occasional flash of wit that I used to relish so, her happy spirit and tough resilience in the face of her continually distressing frustration. I don't *have* to care for her, I *get* to. It is a high honor to care for so wonderful a person.

As a believer in Christ, will you fulfill your sacred vow?

STUDY QUESTIONS

1. If, like the spinning-plates act, your family were an act in a variety show, what would it be?

2. Why do you think the Bible states that God hates divorce? What effects of divorce have you seen in your life or the lives of others?

3. Describe what the phrase "fear God" means to you. What impact does that have on your commitment to God?

4. List ten ways you can tell your wife you love her. What sometimes keeps you from using those ways to communicate that message to her?

5. What would you say are your wife's top three needs right now? How might you serve her to meet those needs better?

6. Reread the words of Robertson McQuilkin on pages 93–94. What's your reaction to his thoughts?

7. How is your relationship with your wife different from the day you married? What can you do this week to make your wife feel like a newlywed again?

CHAPTER SEVEN

COMMITTED TO MARRIAGE

BILL BRIGHT

There once was a man who was very fond of the famous general Robert E. Lee. Every day the man would take his four-year-old son for a stroll through a nearby park, which had a statue of the general mounted atop his beautiful horse, Traveler. And as they walked, he would say to his little lad, "Say good morning to General Lee." And they would say good morning each time they walked by. As the days and weeks passed, the boy got used to the ritual of waving his chubby hand and saying, "Good morning, General Lee." Then one day as they walked past the statue, the boy asked his father, "Daddy, who is that man riding General Lee?"

That story illustrates a tragic fact. There is a tremendous lack of communication in many of our families. All of us who are married remember the day we fell in love. We were ecstatic. Our fiancée was all we could talk about. Then came the marriage vows, and the years passed, and the bloom of marriage passed. And in that process we have a tendency to terminate communication, to no longer listen to one another. The woman who once had the attention of many people now has the inattention of one person: her husband.

Surveys indicate there's very little communication between husbands and wives today, and that is one reason there are so many divorces. In 1945, soon after I became a Christian, a report out of Harvard University indicated that one out of every two and a half marriages ended in divorce—but in only one of 1,015 divorces were the husband and wife both Christians who read the Bible and prayed together daily. Today the divorce rate of Christians is nearly that of non-Christians. It's time we decided as men that we are going to protect our families and divorce-proof our marriages.

I believe there are five commitments that will help you enter into a more vital, dynamic, fulfilling relationship with your wife, if you will faithfully put them into practice. Just as there are laws that govern the whole of creation, so there are laws that govern a happy, meaningful marriage relationship. If we understand how to make marriage work, if we understand that there are laws in our relationships with our wives that are inviolable, just as inviolable as the law of gravity, it will make a vast difference in the success of our marriages.

ACCENTUATE THE POSITIVE

First, commit to concentrating on the attributes of God and on the good qualities of your wife. Many years ago, Dr. James Boice interviewed me on radio nationwide and asked me a question I'd never been asked before: "What is the most important thing you can teach another Christian?" I hadn't had an opportunity to think about it, but out of my innermost being the Holy Spirit answered that question by saying, "The attributes of God." Now that sounds pretty theological, but when you break it down, it's simply an understanding of who is this great God we're here to worship.

God is not "the man upstairs." He is not a divine Santa Claus. He is not a cosmic policeman. He is the One who spoke, and a hundred billion galaxies were flung into space. To give you a little perspective, our planet Earth is like a grain of sand in our galaxy, and our galaxy is no more than a grain of sand in the vastness of all creation. The God who created it all is manifest in the person of Jesus Christ, for He "is the visible expression of the invisible God" (Colossians 1:15, PHILLIPS). He created it all, and the Scripture says He holds it all together by the word of His command.

The Bible commands us to love God with all of our heart, soul, mind, and strength. We're also commanded to love our neighbors, and your closest neighbor is your wife. And we're even commanded to love our enemies! You can't do any of that loving if you haven't first met God.

I was a happy pagan in my youth. I'd been reared in a wonderful home. My mother was a saint; my father wasn't a believer, and I'd grown up on a ranch where my father taught his five sons how to ride the wildest broncos. That does something for your self-image. I thought Christianity was for women like my precious, saintly mother but that men were to be strong and self-reliant. So I went through high school, college, graduate school, a professorship at Oklahoma State University, and then business in Hollywood. Without God, I was my own master, the architect of my own destiny. Then, through my mother's prayers and the influence of the First Presbyterian Church, I met Jesus. I fell in love with Him. He became the most important person in my life.

Very soon I began to understand that all my ways of thinking would be changed. I began to realize the importance of seeking first the kingdom of God and His righteousness, and of laying up treasures in heaven. And the more I learned about Him, the more I realized that God is worthy of my love and my trust and my obedience. So unless one has the right view of who God is— sovereign, righteous, holy, omnipotent, gracious, compassionate—there is a reluctance to say, "Yes, Lord, I will trust You. Yes, Lord, I will love You. Yes, I will obey You." So it is crucial that we understand who God is before we're willing to surrender everything to Him. And in like measure, just as we witness and praise and worship and exalt and honor our great God in words and in holiness of life, we're drawn to Him. Jesus said He would manifest Himself to us if we would obey Him (John 14:23).

In the same way, I'm drawn closer to my beloved, precious Vonette when I praise her for who she is and I thank her for all she does for me. My life has been enriched through the years because of our relationship. We've been married since 1948, so I've had many incredible years of adventure. My life would be a fraction of what it is were it not for her. I look at her and see a woman filled with joy, radiance, and love, who weeps over the needs and souls of people.

As I look at her, I remember what a friend of mine told me years ago. He said that if a woman is beautiful in her teens and twenties, that's the way God made her. But after she's married and the years pass, if she's still beautiful when she's fifty and sixty and seventy, it's because of the way her husband treats her. Think about that a moment. I look at my beautiful wife of forty-nine years and I think, "You're more beautiful than when I married you." And then I remember, according to my friend's illustration, that I've had something to do with it.

I see beautiful, single women who love the Lord and are on the front lines of service but who lose their radiant, joyful countenances after they marry. Why? I believe it's because they aren't encouraged and loved and brought alongside by their husbands. Brother, you can make a difference in your wife. God's Word commands the husband to love his wife as Christ loved the church (Ephesians 5:25). Don't ignore your wife, not even for ministry. Instead, love her as yourself. Just as we need to spend time with God, praising and worshiping Him for who He is and what He has done, thereby drawing us closer to Him, so it is in our relationship with our wives. Make a point every day to spend time praising her and telling her you love her. Make a list of all the good qualities in her life, and thank her for them.

When our children were growing up, I was traveling all over the world, starting this ministry in many countries. Because Vonette and our sons agreed I should do that, we were doing it as a family. Vonette never criticized because she was part of this ministry. As our sons grew to manhood, one of them joined our staff at the University of Washington, and the other became an ordained Presbyterian minister. They love the Lord, and they've often said that I'm their best friend. Who do you think is more responsible than I? Their mother. She never criticized. She never found fault. She knew that she was number one in my life. We determined when we married that divorce would never be an option and that we would never criticize each other. We would never go to bed with any kind of unresolved conflict. Every day I call her just to ask, "How are you doing? Just want you to know I love you. You're wonderful." I often introduce her as my beautiful, charming, adorable wife, and that embarrasses her. But I mean it. You see, marriage is for keeps if we follow the commands of Scripture.

Your partner is for a lifetime, until death do you part, so why not enjoy her? Why not work at this matter of helping her to be God's maximum woman? Vonette is the most important person in my life, apart from the Lord Jesus Christ. And even though I spend more time on planes than I generally do in my bed at home, I have found that concentrating on helping my precious wife be the woman God created her to be is the most profitable investment of my time. And so I cannot overemphasize the importance of taking another look at your wife. If for some reason she is dowdy and glum and depressed and discouraged, look in the mirror, and find out who is the major contributor to her looks. And then begin to cultivate her with love. You don't have to spend a lot of money; just let her know you love her in a thousand different ways. And before long, that dull countenance will become radiant and will be filled with joy, and out of her innermost being there will be tremendous blessing.

I can tell you that if Vonette were unhappy, it would rob me of my ministry for the Lord. If she were not walking with Christ, I would be hindered, inhibited. But she walks with God. She is my number-one disciple. Of all the thousands of men and women whose lives I've poured my love and prayers into, Vonette is my number-one disciple. And your wife is your number-one disciple.

SURRENDER TO CHRIST

Second, if you're going to have a maximum marriage, make a total and irrevocable commitment to the lordship of Jesus Christ, individually and as a couple. When I proposed to Vonette, I promised her the world, and she believed me. But after we had been married about two years, though both of us were very materialistic, we began to grow in Christ, and we saw the truth of what Jesus taught: Seek first the kingdom of God and lay up treasures in heaven. So one Sunday afternoon in 1951, we decided to sign a contract with Jesus in which we relinquished all of our rights and all of our possessions to preach God's good news. Forty-six years ago we became the slaves of Jesus. It was only two or three nights later when, through a miraculous vision of God, He spoke to me while I was studying for one of my final exams at Fuller Seminary and gave me a vision we now call Campus Crusade for Christ. That vision is to help take the gospel to every person on planet Earth in this generation. And, by God's grace, many tens of thousands have joined me in that commitment.

I seriously doubt that God would have entrusted me with that vision had I not signed that contract with Him. When Vonette and I put our names to it, we were thinking of the passage in Mark 8, where Jesus said to the disciples, "If any man would come after me, let him deny himself and take up his cross and follow me" (8:34, RSV). That sounded like a hard saying, but I must tell you, as Jesus goes on to say, that if you insist on saving your life, you will lose it. "Only those who throw away their lives for my sake and for the sake of the Good News will ever know what it means to really live" (8:35, TLB). I can tell you, since that contract was signed—that total, irrevocable surrender to His lordship—we have known adventure. Problems? Yes, by the score. But always with us was the living Christ, in whom dwells all the fullness of the Godhead bodily, indwelling us, and He is the source of our wisdom and love and grace. If you've not yet surrendered your life fully to Christ and abdicated the throne of your life to His control, I strongly encourage you to do that today. Our Lord set an example by coming to earth disguised as a slave (Philippians 2), and the apostle Paul viewed himself as a slave of Jesus (Romans 1:1). So should we surrender our lives to God as His slaves.

COMMIT TO EACH OTHER

Third, to ensure a maximum marriage, make a firm commitment to each other. In Ephesians 5 we're told, "Be not drunk with wine, wherein is excess; but be filled with the Spirit" (5:18, KJV). When we're filled with the Spirit, we will sing and make melody in our hearts to the Lord, wives will fit in with their husbands' plans, and husbands will show the same kind of love to their wives that Christ showed to the church by giving Himself totally for her.

In 1 Corinthians 13 we have an insight into what that means. Love as expressed in Scripture is an expression of the will. If I truly love Vonette, I will be kind to her, because the Scripture says love will act kindly. Love is pure. Love always seeks ways to make itself strong on behalf of others. If you love someone, you'll always be loyal to that person. And though you speak with the tongue of men and angels, or have the gift of prophecy to know all things, without love there is no value to your gift. You can even give your body to be burned, but without love it is of no value whatever.

Some years ago I was going through a tremendous personnel crisis with some beloved staff members into whom I'd poured my life, wonderful men whom I loved dearly. God spoke to me one night, about two o'clock in the morning, and for the next two hours He showed me how to love by faith. Always remember: The command of God is to love. There's no question about it. You're not only to love God but your neighbor. You're to love your enemies. There are no exceptions. You cannot do it in the flesh, but with God's enabling through His Holy Spirit, you can love by faith. Claim this promise from 1 John 5:14–15: If we ask anything according to His will, He hears and answers us. Make a list of everybody with whom you're having trouble. If it's your coworkers or family members, add them to the list. If there is a conflict with your wife, place her at the top of your list. Then begin to say, "O God, I claim Your supernatural love for this person. I want to be patient and kind, never jealous or envious or boastful or proud, never haughty or selfish or rude." Make a commitment to love others.

If you have a problem with praying, it may be because of your relationship with your wife. Listen to this: "You husbands must be careful of your wives, being thoughtful of their needs and honoring them as the weaker sex. Remember that you and your wife are partners in receiving God's blessings, and if you don't treat her as you should, your prayers will not get ready answers" (1 Peter 3:7, TLB). It is impossible for God to hear and answer your prayers if you have sin in your heart. And if you're not treating your mate as she should be treated, God cannot bless you or your marriage.

COMMIT TO THE SPIRITUAL DISCIPLINES

Fourth, for a maximum marriage, make a commitment to the Word of God, to prayer, fasting, and a godly life. The world is seeking to invade our minds. Everything about us is under constant attack by the ways of the world. With all of the pornography and other kinds of filth available, one has to be truly disciplined. So hide the Word of God in your heart and, husbands, pray and seek God's face together with your wife. God will answer as you unite. Vonette and I begin every day in prayer, as we have since we were first engaged, and we end every day on our knees in prayer together. Whenever I'm alone, I do the same, and she also, because to bow and acknowledge together our great God as Lord and Master greatly enhances our relationship.

Find a Bible you can read in a single year. Spend fifteen or twenty minutes a day, and you can read the whole Bible in a year.

Vonette and I read God's Word daily. She has one translation and I another so that we get the rich, rewarding experience of God's Word.

Pray and fast together. I went through a forty-day fast last summer, and I was greatly encouraged the last two weeks of my fast when Vonette joined with me to pray for revival in America and the world and to pray for the fulfillment of the Great Commission. By God's grace, we're sensing a mighty movement of the Spirit throughout the world. There's never been such a great spiritual harvest as is taking place today. More people are hearing the gospel. More people are receiving Christ. More people are being trained to serve Christ than at any time in history. God is preparing us for a harvest that will enable us to see the fulfillment of the Great Commission, and literally hundreds of millions of people will come into the kingdom. I believe the men's movement is one of the most significant evidences of revival and awakening in our country, and as we begin living godly lives and being the kind of fathers and husbands God has called us to be, spiritual revival will continue to accelerate and spread.

LIVE IN THE POWER OF THE SPIRIT

Finally, for a maximum marriage we need to commit to live moment by moment in the power of the Holy Spirit. Apart from His enabling, we cannot be good husbands, we cannot be good fathers, we cannot be honest and truthful; for the Spirit of God is the only One who can help us to be all that God has commanded. I have known what it means to live in the energy of the flesh. I know what Romans 7 is all about: "O wretched man that I am!" (7:24, KJV). I know what 1 Corinthians 3 is all about, where Paul refers to people as being baby Christians—carnal, fleshly, and worldly. But now I know the joy of walking day by day in the power of the Holy Spirit.

That doesn't mean I'm a perfect husband or that I don't make mistakes. Only a short time ago I became a little impatient about the fact that whenever I wanted to cut anything, our knives were dull. So I decided to buy several knives that never have to be sharpened. I brought them home, and Vonette said, "Take them back. We don't need them."

"But all our knives are dull," I protested. Pretty soon we were in conflict. But then we both realized how foolish we were, we both confessed that we were expressing our own fleshly, carnal desires, and we each asked the other to forgive. So she gave me the knives for Christmas, and I gave her a knife sharpener. And we lived happily ever after.

There have been plenty of times when I've not been the perfect husband nor she the perfect wife, but we know a concept: "If we confess our sins, he is faithful and just to forgive us our sins, and to cleanse us from all unrighteousness" (1 John 1:9, KJV). Every time you're angry with your wife, or impatient, or unkind, ask the Holy Spirit to cleanse you of that attitude. If you're a believer, the Holy Spirit already dwells within you. He came to dwell within you the moment you received Christ. Father, Son, and Holy Spirit now reside in your body, a temple of God. But unless you allow Him, He will have no power to perform what He is commanded to do. The last words our Lord spoke before He ascended to the Father were, "You will receive power when the Holy Spirit comes on you; and you will be my witnesses" (Acts 1:8). And the only way my wife and I can be true witnesses is by walking in the fullness of the Spirit every day.

You cannot be a good husband or a good father apart from the enabling of the Holy Spirit. If you become aware of an attitude or an action in your life that is displeasing to the Lord, even though you are walking with Him and sincerely desiring to serve Him, simply thank God that He has forgiven your sins—past, present, and future—on the basis of Christ's death on the cross. Claim His love and forgiveness by faith, and continue to have fellowship with Him.

If you retake the throne of your life through sin (a definite act of disobedience), *breathe* spiritually. Spiritual breathing is an exercise of faith that enables you to experience God's love and forgiveness. Simply exhale the impure and inhale the pure.

To exhale, you must confess your sin. Agree with God concerning your sin, and thank Him for His forgiveness of it, according to 1 John 1:9 and Hebrews 10:1–25. Confession involves repentance, which means there will be a change in your attitude and your action. Confess your sin to God and exhale all those impurities from your life.

To inhale, surrender the control of your life to Christ, and receive the fullness of the Holy Spirit by faith. Trust that He now directs and empowers you, according to the command of Ephesians 5:18 and the promise of 1 John 5:14–15. Make this your prayer: "Holy Spirit of God, fill me with Your power. Help me to be a better husband, a better father. Help me to reach out to share your love and forgiveness in Christ with others. Now, by faith, I claim the fullness of the Holy Spirit."

STUDY QUESTIONS

1. If you couldn't use words, how would you communicate the message "You're great!" to your wife? What does your typical non-verbal communication at home say about your opinion of your wife?

2. What do you like best about your wife? When are you tempted to overlook those qualities? What can you do about that?

3. Why do you suppose a commitment to Christ makes a difference in a marriage?

4. How does a man demonstrate commitment to Christ in real, tangible ways?

5. Finish this sentence: "If my commitment to spiritual disciplines were an omelet, it would look like..."

6. What makes it difficult for you to rely completely on the Holy Spirit to enable you to be committed to your marriage?

7. What can you do to remind your wife of your commitment to her and your marriage? When will you do it?

CHAPTER EIGHT

IMITATING THE FATHER

JOE STOWELL

O f all the tragedies in the social revolution in America, there is no tragedy greater than the fact we have put our children at risk like no generation before. This is a society ruled by the powerful and those who hold position, and the weak go wanting. And the weak in our day are the children of our cities, our streets, and our homes.

I have been touched by two indelible experiences in recent years—one of those experiences you no doubt remember. We saw a fireman hold a child in his arms, bleeding from the Oklahoma City bombing. As I watched, I thought, "What has happened to our world that we would put our children at risk to random, senseless violence?"

The other experience was closer to home, as one Tuesday afternoon I took off my tie and jacket and went with five of our students to the neighboring community in Chicago known as Cabrini Green. It's what Harlem is to New York and Watts is to Los Angeles. These five students were part of one hundred and fifty who run our Big Brother/Big Sister program, and I told them I wanted to walk through the projects with them. Walking into that area of Chicago was like walking into a war zone. Six thousand people live in Cabrini Green, forty-five hundred of them children—children who become sexually active at the ages of eleven and twelve. For young girls, the highest badge of status is to get pregnant and have a child. Most have no fathers. Children are surrounded by gangs, as though they are under siege. They realize they can make more money selling drugs on the corner than flipping hamburgers at McDonald's. These children are at phenomenal risk.

Meanwhile, most of us are saying, "Well, we don't live in that kind of a neighborhood." The fact is, if our children live in this world, they live in a nasty neighborhood. They are not safe when they bury their ears under the headphones of their Walkman and listen to their music. They are not safe when they flip on the television or plug in their videos. They are not safe when they go to school where God is out and condoms are in. We live in a Beavis and Butthead world, a world not safe for our children. A standard is being raised by the enemy of their souls, and on this battlefield God is looking for a few good men who will change all that and raise the standard of Christ for their children.

I don't know of a more challenging task than to be a father.

SEIZE THE DAY

I'm no expert on fathering; I'm a co-struggler. I understand the pressures of raising kids in this world. James Dobson says rearing children is like trying to nail Jell-O to the wall. In fact, parenting is the spookiest business in the whole world. When Martie and I were trying to work through this parenting maze and things got really tough at home, at times we would just look at each other and say, "This too shall pass." And then it did pass. We're in the empty-nest season now, and when I look in the rearview mirror, I feel some regret. But it's time for those of you who are busy parenting right now to seize the day.

When my oldest son was big enough to play basketball, I went out and bought a nice new basketball set with the pole and the backboard and the rim. We dug a hole, mixed the cement, and put the backboard right at the end of the driveway. It raised my son's expectations that Dad was going to play basketball with him. But whenever I had leisure time at home, I wanted to work on my lawn. I'm a lawnaholic. I like ours to be the greenest, most manicured, best-looking lawn on the block. In my work, I'm never done with anything. I can never finish a task. But I can go home and cut the lawn, then sit back and say, "There. I did it." For a year and a half, every time Joe wanted to play basketball, I was busy working in the yard.

I was a pastor at the time, and I remember driving home one day from the funeral of a sixteen-year-old boy in our church, thinking about what a treasure our children are. As I turned the corner and drove down our street, there was my lawn. It was the trimmest, greenest, best lawn on the block. I remember pulling into the driveway, and there at the end of the driveway was the basketball hoop. Suddenly my lawn became a symbol of sorrow. I thought of all the times Joe had asked me to play ball with him and I said, "Not now. I'm too busy." I got out of the car, went through the front door, and yelled, "Joe!"

"What?" came the answer from his room.

"Joe!" I shouted. "Let's play basketball."

And he answered, "Dad, I'm busy."

I had lost the season. There is a Latin phrase for what we are to do: *carpe diem.* "Seize the day." Now is the time to seize the day for our children.

EMBRACE THE RESPONSIBILITY

Ephesians 6:4 begins with the word "Fathers." It's kind of a lonely verse, I think. I wish it said, "Fathers, mothers, pastors, friends, grandparents, neighbors, and anybody you can find, get together and do this task." Instead it just says, "Fathers, father your children."

I think it's interesting that if you've had children, you're a father whether you like it or not. God gave us three children. I didn't choose them, God did. It's the same for all parents. In the same way, our kids are born into a family. They get us. They don't get to choose. The issue is not, will we be fathers? The issue is, what kind of fathers will we be? Ephesians calls on us to embrace the responsibility. "Fathers," it says, "here's your responsibility."

Those of us who work in management are constantly told to *simplify the task.* Get it down to the three or four things that only you can do, then give the rest away. The same thing is true of fathering. Where does fathering fit in your responsibilities? Is it on the short list of those few things only you can do? Nobody else can be a father to my kids but me. I don't know why I ever thought, "Ha! I'll earn the money, she'll raise the kids!" That's not right. I've got to embrace the responsibility. Fathering has to be on the short list of things only I can do.

I'll never forget opening the mail one day when I had been at Moody only three or four months. There was an anonymous letter signed "redrum" at the bottom. "Redrum" is "murder" spelled backwards, and a movie at the time featured that violent example in its plot. The letter said, "If the Moody Bible Institute doesn't make a hundred-thousand-dollar contribution to the New York Times Homeless Fund within seven days, we will take your life. In fact…we would probably rather take your life than get your money."

That was an unsettling piece of mail, needless to say, but I thought, "Just some quack." However, one of my associates told me we ought to take it to the Chicago police. Unfortunately they said, "We've studied this letter. You need to take it seriously." That changed seven days of my life. The police said, "Don't tell your family; there's no use upsetting them." Then they got the local police to guard the house, driving up and down our street. (Afterward my wife said she couldn't understand why we had such great attention from the police!)

I remember on the seventh day I was about to get in my car to go home when suddenly I thought, "I don't want to open my car door. What if it's rigged and bombed?" I considered calling one of my assistants, "Here! Take my car!" Thankfully, it didn't explode, and I drove out of the little parking lot breathing easier. As I was driving home, I realized this might be my last night with my family. It's fascinating how that changed my entire perspective.

My youngest son, Matt, had been asking me to take him bowling. Bowling has never been my favorite sport. I'd been putting him off for months. But that night I rolled up to the house, thinking, "I'm taking Matthew bowling tonight!" Fathering got short-listed right away.

I walked in the door and called out, "Matt, what are you doing tonight?"

He said, "Nothing, Dad."

"Let's go bowling," I suggested.

"Great!" he responded.

Then Martie gave me this look. "Bowling? We were going to take him shopping for school clothes tonight."

Now, next to bowling my second least favorite sport is shopping. But I said to her, "Well, let's go bowling first, and then we'll go to T. J. Maxx." So we bowled frame after frame. I shelled out pockets full of quarters for him to play the video games. Then we were off to the store, and I was helping pick out clothes and taking him on several trips to the dressing room. Matt had all my attention.

What made the difference? When I thought about the critical nature of fathering and realized it might be my last night, fathering made it to the top of my "To Do" list. A friend of mine once said, "No man on his deathbed ever wished he had spent more time in the office." If somebody said to you, "What are the few things that only you can do?" I wonder if you would reply, "Well, one of them is being a father to my kids. And I'm trying to give everything else away." Fathers who raise the standard of Christ embrace that responsibility and put fathering on their short list.

DELETE THE DESTRUCTIVE

Ephesians 6:4 poses a strategic warning to fathers: Delete the destructive. It literally reads, "Fathers, do not bring anger up alongside of your children." I'm not sure we understand how destructive anger is in the hearts of our children. There are few forces more debilitating than an angry spirit. When children are angry with their parents, they withdraw. They become quiet. They slam shut all of the doors to their ears, minds, and hearts toward their parents. Do you ever wonder why some children choose all the wrong friends? Sometimes it's because they're so angry with their parents they don't want to spend time in their parents' world. They will do anything they can to embarrass their parents, to get back at their dads. Sometimes smart kids, intellectually solid kids, get bad grades just to make a statement to their parents. Daughters may get pregnant to make a statement. When our children become angry in their spirits, we have made them vulnerable to destructive forces in their lives. It's no wonder our Father in heaven says to us, "When you father, don't bring anger up alongside your children."

One of the things that brings anger alongside our children is breaking promises consistently. When we raise our children's expectations, they begin counting on us, and then when we don't keep our promises, they're disappointed. If that happens over and over again, they become discouraged. Then they despair. Pretty soon their spirits begin to sour. When our children ask us for something, they consider any answer short of an absolute no as a yes. If you say, "Well, maybe…we'll see," they're in! So buck up.

Say no more often if you can't keep the promise.

Just as broken promises are a source of disappointment, so is publicly embarrassing our children in front of their brothers and sisters or their friends. Comparing them to others can also sour their spirits. Think of the impact in a child's life when we say, "Why can't you be more like Lisa? She's so pretty and smart."

When we ignore our kids, we create anger. I doubt there's a worse insult in the world than being ignored. I'd rather be punched in the nose. At least I'm worth the expenditure of your energy. But to ignore our children when they need us sets them up for anger. I learned, probably a little too late, that my children are not impressed with my office. My kids are not impressed with my schedule outside of the home. I've written a whole bunch of books, and my kids haven't read one of them. Do you know how discouraging that is? I learned that my kids are only impressed with my time and attention. That's it. That's all they need. That's all they want—my time and attention.

A famous football coach in the NFL who, by his own admission, literally gave his whole life to football and consciously, volitionally neglected his family and his children met his son coming in the door late one night. This coach said to him, "Why are you late? Where have you been?" The boy exploded on the spot. "Dad, the question is not where have I been! The question is 'Where have you been?'"

We neglect our children at our peril.

Another big error is failing to admit mistakes. We think if we admit to our kids and our wives that we're wrong, they'll stop respecting us. That's dumb. They already know we made a mistake. All they want to hear from us is "I was wrong. I don't want to be that kind of dad. I don't want to be that kind of husband." They want us to humble ourselves and ask for their forgiveness.

And one of the great things about kids is they never put you on probation. I have never gone to my kids and asked forgiveness only to have them say, "Oh yeah? I'll give you six months." Every time, they throw their arms around my neck and say, "Oh Dad, that's all right. We all make mistakes. I love you." It's a wonderful thing to realize that our kids want to love us, they want to respect us, they want a relationship with us. They just may be the only people in the world who *want* to love you, who *want* to respect you. With everyone else you have to *work* for those things. When we come to our kids and apologize, they want to repair the relationship with us. But when we refuse to humble ourselves, when we break our promises, when we publicly embarrass them or compare them or abuse them or ignore them, then anger begins to sour their souls. We have to take the steps to resolve these problems, lest the destructive force of anger begins to consume them and puts them at risk.

TOUCH THE DIVINE

We are not only to delete that which is destructive, but when God calls us to fatherhood, He tells us to share with them the touch of the divine. Delight their lives with the divine. The text goes on to say, "Fathers, do not bring anger up alongside your children, but bring them up in the discipline and instruction of the Lord." The little phrase "of the Lord" is the most important phrase in the whole verse. It means I am to father my children in ways consistent with Christ's way. I am to treat my children the way the Lord treats me. I am to father my children the way God fathers me. I am to bring them up by letting them be delighted with the touch of the divine from their dad. The word translated "to bring them up" literally means "to nurture them" or "to get them out." As I said before, Martie and I are in the empty-nest season of life. If we had known how good this phase is, we'd have kicked our kids out when they were ten!

Erma Bombeck said that rearing children is like flying a kite. You let out a little string, and it gets caught in the trees. And you let out a little more, and it gets caught in the wires. And you let out a little more, until eventually the day comes when you have to let the string go. The call to us fathers is to bring them up and send them out, but to do it in a way that they leave having seen the heavenly Father in their own father and knowing they will go on with their heavenly Father because their earthly dad did.

To begin revealing God to your kids, do what the Lord does. First, He convinces me that He is always there for me—in His forgiving power and with all His resources. He says to me, "I will never leave thee, nor forsake thee" (Hebrews 13:5, KJV). When is the last time you wrapped your arms around your kids and said, "I want you to know that no matter what happens, I will be there for you, and I will be there to help you. I will take all the resources and all of my power to come alongside of your life"? Early in life they go everywhere with you. Then they grow up a little bit and don't want to go anyplace with you anymore, but you have to go with them because they can't drive themselves. You attend stuff like elementary band concerts and ball games. Just showing up is a way to convince them of the fact "I'll be with you." When my boys were playing basketball, as they warmed up before the game, they may have been looking at the coach or glancing at the hoop, but they were also gazing at the door to see if Dad was going to walk through.

Our Lord not only convinces us of His presence and His resources. He touches us with His full forgiveness. He also teaches, advises, warns, and guides us through His Word. When was the last time you told your children, "One of my purposes in life is to teach you everything I know about life"? Begin to feed them truth, like the fact that success is not how much you make but how much you please the Father. Help your sons understand that women are not to be used for a man's own pleasure but are to be valued and treasured as cherished colleagues on the pathway of life. When was the last time you told your children you wanted to teach them everything you knew to be true from God? When was the last time you warned them and made their boundaries clear?

I remember one time a man came to me and said, "Pastor, I've got a big problem. My daughter does everything wrong. I had no idea the teenage years were going to be like this." And he went through his whole list of everything she had done wrong.

So I asked him, "Have you ever told your daughter what you expect of her?"

I couldn't believe his answer: "Well, no, as a matter of fact I haven't."

So I'm thinking, "Where did you expect her to get it? By osmosis in your house?" Then I had teenagers, and I found myself saying, "They just ought to know those kinds of things!" Christ not only convinces us of His presence, He teaches us and warns us and guides us.

He also affirms our worth and value. I have a friend who used to get in bed with his kids on a periodic basis and say to them, "You know, if we lined up every eight-year-old along the horizon, and your mother and I walked by them all, we'd keep looking until we finally found you, and then we'd pick you out of all the eight-year-olds in the whole wide world." His kids would break out in a smile as they fell asleep because he affirmed their worth and their value.

Jesus Christ came and affirmed my worth and my value. If I were the only one to live on this planet, He would have come to die for me. Affirm the worth and value of your children by serving them. They're not here to serve us; we are here to serve them.

And Christ meets us where we are. Instead of waiting for us to get perfect, Christ decided to come and meet us where we are. He didn't stand on the edge of heaven and yell down, "Hey! Come on up!" He got out of His place and came down to meet me in my place. And He takes me by the hand and leads me back to His place. I couldn't get there unless He came to meet me.

I used to think my kids would love to spend a day at the office with me, so I'd say, "Hey, you've got the day off from school. Let's go to the office." They always replied, "Thanks, Dad. I've got something else to do." That's when I realized I had to go into *their* world to meet them where they are—which at times can be a real struggle. For example, I hate board games, but I had three kids who loved them, and I had to go into their world. So it was Chutes and Ladders on the living room rug. Later it was skateboards and roller blades. We father our children like Christ ministers to us, by meeting them in their world.

There is one more thing God does that we ought to emulate. He envisions a glorious future for us. He says to us, "Take heart. Soon this life will be over. There are many mansions in my Father's house. I go to prepare a place for you, and if I go to prepare a place for you, I will come again and receive you unto Myself, that where I am there you may be also" (see John 14:1–3). He envisions a glorious future for us. Fathers, we have to envision a glorious future for our children. We have to believe in them and their potential. We have to tell them they can be used by God and be effective on this planet.

I remember praying with my son Matthew, "Dear Lord, help Matthew grow up to be a man of God." Every night I'd pray that. And one day my son said, "Dad, can I pray?" Then he bowed his head and said, "Lord, help me to grow up to be a man of God." A vision for a glorious future.

Our children will think of their Father in heaven in terms of what kind of a father we have been to them. Early in our marriage, my wife and I decided to pay cash for things and not rob God of the opportunity of meeting our needs. So God tested us. We had this little beat-up Volkswagen, and one of the front tires had about an eighth of an inch of rubber dust between the air and the road. Normally we would have gone down and flashed the card to get a new tire. But we were committed to waiting on God to supply our needs. Our oldest son was about four then, and we said, "Joe, God has promised to supply all of our needs, and we are going to pray that He will help us have the money for a new tire."

He looked at me and said, "Dad, don't bother. God's too busy drinking Pepsi."

I'm sitting there thinking, "Where did you get a theology like that? You didn't learn that in this house." Then I realized we'd been teaching this boy to pray "Dear heavenly Father," and I was the only father he knew. Maybe it was the time his bike broke down, and he came to me while I was drinking Pepsi and reading the newspaper, and when he asked me to help him with his bike, I said, "Not now, uh, I'm...I'm too busy."

Our sons and daughters will look at us as fathers and envision that their Father in heaven is like their father on earth. That's why God says we must treat our children the way the Lord treats us. Delight their lives with a touch of the divine.

RAISE THE STANDARD

When Matt was just a little boy, I left for a seventeen-day trip to Africa. After Martie and the kids kissed me good-bye, Matt cried all the way home. He refused to be comforted.

He finally sobbed, "Mom, you don't understand. If Daddy's plane crashes, who will wrestle with me?"

What a shock. I thought I was here for the shoes and the food on the table and the clothes and the mortgage. But what mattered most to my son was who would wrestle with him.

That's when I realized that I raise the standard of Christ for my children through everything I do. Being a good father isn't an issue of what kind of a parent I am; being a good father is an issue of what kind of a person I am. Are we fathers submitted to the Lord Christ in our lives? If so, the love, character, and quality of Christ will flow through our lives. The standard of Christ will be raised. Our children will be delighted by the touch of the divine, and we will have deleted that which would destroy them.

I'm an incurable people person, but you need to know that sometimes even "people" people get "peopled" out. I got in the car one evening after a day's work, and I was so thankful just to be alone. I decided that when I got home I'd head straight for the closet and tell my wife, "Slide the newspaper and supper under the door, and don't speak to me for three hours." You know that feeling?

But about halfway home, God started to work me over. "I called you to those *people* at home—your wife and kids." I thought about the fact that all they want is my time and my attention. Frankly, I struggled with the thought of denying myself and getting back into the people business again. As I drove into the driveway that night, I knew Martie would want a piece of my life, and my kids would want to get down on the floor and wrestle.

So I walked into the kitchen, leaned back on the counter, and said, "Hey, Martie, let's talk about each other's day. How did your day go? Tell me every detail." I thought she would faint. We talked, and then I volunteered to get the kids out from underfoot. The kids and I went out and wrestled on the floor. That's not what I wanted to do, but when I put my head on the pillow that night, I was thankful Martie hadn't rolled over thinking, "Why doesn't he ever talk to me?" And my kids weren't going to sleep saying, "Why doesn't Dad ever pay attention to us?" I knew that if God had walked into my home that night, He would have gone straight to the kitchen to be with Martie and would have wanted to wrestle with the kids.

If we are to raise the standard of Christ for our children, then we must raise the Lordship of Christ in our lives. If we do that, we will rescue our children from the risk and danger that surrounds them.

STUDY QUESTIONS

1. How do you think your children would describe you? What would they say are your dominant qualities?

2. If you knew you had only one week to live, what would you do with your children? How is that similar to or different from what you do with your children right now?

3. What can we do to be more consistent in keeping our promises to our children? What's the best thing to do when we discover we've broken a promise to a child?

4. What elements of your lifestyle have a negative impact on your relationship with your children? How can you "delete the destructive" in those cases?

5. In what way is God most like a father to you? How can you reflect that kind of fatherhood to your own children?

6. What dreams do you have for your children's future? How are you communicating those hopes and expectations to them?

7. Why are men often distracted from spending time and energy with their children? What can you do this week to overcome those distractions?

CHAPTER NINE

LEAVING A LEGACY

BRUCE WILKINSON

Thirty years ago at a conference in the Northeast, I found out that a man sitting off to the side was the son of a very famous Christian leader. Being much younger then, I decided to introduce myself and find out what it was like to grow up in his father's home. I worked my way over to him and said, "I understand that you're such-and-such, the son of so-and-so." He stared at me. Then I said, "What was it like, growing up in your father and mother's home? What was it like being the son of such a great Christian leader?" The next thing I knew, that man turned, swore at me, swore at his father, swore about the Bible, and said, "I hate God. I hate Jesus Christ." Then he turned on his heel and walked out of that conference, and didn't come back the rest of the day.

You could have picked me off the ground. All I could think about at that moment was "How could this possibly be? How could a son of such a godly leader be so rebellious?" And I remember saying to myself that I couldn't think of anything worse than to have my son or my daughter swear about God and about Jesus Christ. I couldn't think of anything more gut-wrenching than to have my children hate me. What had happened, and what could I do to avoid it happening in my family?

THE THREE CHAIRS

Then the Lord revealed to me in Scripture what I am to do to prevent that from happening. Imagine there are three chairs. Each of them represents something that has profound implications for your life. In Joshua chapter 24, you can see a man who sits in the first chair. His name is Joshua, and in the last chapter of the book he says, "But as for me and my house, we will serve the LORD" (Joshua 24:15, NKJV). Here is a man willing to make a promise. I want to put Joshua in the first chair, as a person who is committed to God. Those who remain close to Him sit in the first chair.

But of the generation that outlives Joshua, there is another description. In Joshua 24:31 it says, "Israel served the LORD all the days of Joshua" [that's generation one] "and all the days of the elders who outlived Joshua, who had known all the works of the LORD which He had done for Israel" (NKJV)—that's the second generation. The first generation is the generation of Joshua. They had seen God work in their midst, and they were committed to Him. The second generation includes those who outlived Joshua. They knew about the works God had done for Israel.

If you skip a couple of pages in your Bible, you'll find the people who grew up in those second-generation homes. In Judges 2:10 we read, "When all that generation had been gathered to their fathers, another generation arose after them who did not know the LORD nor the work which He had done for Israel" (NKJV). The first generation *knew God*. The second generation *knew about God*. The third generation *did not know God*.

The person who sits in the first chair knows the Lord

intimately, the one in the second chair also knows the Lord but only on the surface, and the one in the third chair does not know the Lord. In a sense, the three chairs represent the grandparents, the parents, and the children. The grandchildren of Joshua didn't know the Lord. They were not born-again. Just two generations later! Who would have believed it? The Bible says the first generation knew the Lord and the second generation knew the Lord, but the third generation knew *not* the Lord. The first was saved, the second was saved, but the third was *not* saved.

Note also that the first generation *had the works*; they saw the tremendous miracles God did for Israel. They experienced the power of God in their lives. They committed themselves to God, saying, "I'm going to serve God. As for me and my house, we will serve the Lord." When God hears that from a man's heart, God responds. He answers the prayer, and He moves mightily. When you live in a home that's committed to God, whose father is the leader of the home, whose father's heart cries out to God, "As for me and my house, yes! We will serve the Lord," you are naturally drawn to become a believer.

The second generation did not have the works, but they had *seen and heard about* the works God had done. They knew of the mighty miracles God had performed for the first generation. They just hadn't ever experienced that power firsthand.

If you were to track it down, you would find that young people who have grown up in a Christian home often can't remember a time they didn't believe in Jesus. I was fortunate enough to grow up in a home with parents who were born-again.

My parents were sold out to Jesus, and as far back as I can remember, I always believed in Jesus Christ. I saw my parents' faith and was attracted to it. It was winsome. It was wonderful. It was life changing. It was powerful. I couldn't help but follow as our father led our house and followed the Lord. When you grow up in a committed home, you know about the Lord.

But unless you develop a faith of your own, unless you come to know the Lord for yourself, you're not going to be as committed as your parents. That's the downside of the second chair.

I'm convinced that the majority of American churches are filled with men who sit in the second chair. They know who they ought to be, they know how they ought to live, but they aren't really committed to Christ. He isn't as real to them as He was to their parents. They haven't seen Him work miracles the way their parents did. So their faith gets soft. If the first chair is marked by *commitment,* the second chair is marked by *compromise.* Sometimes they talk about God, and sometimes they walk with God, but most of the time God takes second place in their lives. He is pushed out by their own needs and desires. They start focusing on acquiring material things, and their walk with God becomes a Sunday routine. There's no fire in their faith, and that coolness is passed on to their children.

That third generation grows up in a home that has backed away from God. And those children sense that God isn't really very important to their parents, so they will often rebel against everything their parents stand for. They sit in the third chair, far away from the Lord.

The tragic thing about the third-chair grandchildren of Joshua is that the Bible says they *knew not* the Lord. They weren't saved. More shocking than that, they didn't even know about the miracles that had been done for Joshua's generation! They didn't know about the miracle at Jericho. They didn't know about the sun standing still. They didn't know about the manna, or the quail, or the water from the rock. They didn't know about the Jordan opening. And why not? Because their parents, the second generation, who had heard about the works but didn't have works in their own lives, never told them. They didn't want to talk about the miracles of the previous generation. Why? Because then their children would want to know, "Dad, why don't we have any miracles like that in our home? Why isn't God real here? Where are the great stories of God's power in our own generation?"

THE CHURCH AND THE CHAIR

One generation knows the Lord, the next knows about Him, and the third doesn't know Him at all. The first has the works, the second knows about the works, and the third never even hears about the works. The first generation is marked by commitment; they are going to serve the Lord. The second chair is marked by compromise. They're going to serve themselves. The third is marked by confusion; they don't know what to believe! When you grow up in a compromising home, you're going to have conflict all of your life. Sometimes you're going to try to live this way, and later you'll try to live that way. But you're going to have a divided mind, and you're going to say throughout your life, "I just can't seem to find myself." You don't find a second-chair person saying that. And the first-chair people have forgotten about themselves and focused on the Lord. But this third generation doesn't know who they are or what they believe.

What's true of people is also true of churches. Some churches are in the first chair, experiencing the power of God. People are being saved, prayer is powerful, and people are joyfully worshiping the Lord. Some churches are in the second chair, believing in God and the Bible but not really seeing any power in their lives. They are more concerned with how things look, so they build bigger buildings and buy bigger organs. They wear nice suits and drive nice cars. Then there is the third-chair church, which doesn't even know what's true. They're in a constant state of revising the truth so they can try to feel good about themselves.

I believe one of the crucial tasks of the men's movement is to get men to move to the first chair. They go to conferences and ask, "Can I ever get to the first chair? What's it going to take, God?" But God is clear. It's going to take a decision on your part to commit wholeheartedly to the Lord.

Every Christian family starts out in the first chair. Every denomination does, too. Abraham sat in the first chair, honoring God with his life. But then you look at his son, Isaac, and you find a man full of compromise. And Isaac's son Jacob tried to cheat everyone, tried to get ahead, and even tried to manipulate God. He was a man in conflict, until he eventually turned to the Lord.

You see, the first chair is a chair that puts God first: "As for me and my house, we *will serve* the LORD." When you grow up in a

God-centered home, you're going to come to know the Lord. You can't help it. It's wonderful. It's the blessing of God on the home. That blessing is going to ooze over to your young life, and you're going to naturally begin your life living on the faith of your parents. You're going to soak in their confidence in the Lord, their strength, their commitment, and their values. You're going to share your parents' values.

But as you grow, there will come a time when you will have to make a choice. Are you going to stay in the second chair, or are you going to move? Because what happens as you get older is that your vocabulary moves from "God and me" to "me and God." Unfortunately, it sometimes becomes just "me." You say to yourself, "I'm going to do what I want. Come on, God. Come with me and, please, bless me."

That's what the second chair looks like, but when you grow up in a chair that has a me-and-God focus, you're going to have trouble in your life as a third-chair person. You'll begin to notice that your parents, who live in the second chair, *look* the part because you can't tell the difference between a second-chair person and a first-chair person by appearance. In fact, second-chair people even look *better* than first-chair believers in many cases! They often have nicer clothes, carry a bigger Bible, and might even know more Bible facts because they grew up going to Sunday school each week.

But when you live in that third chair, you unfortunately may watch mom and dad verbally fight all the way to church. Until you pull into the church parking lot, that is, and something all of a sudden comes over your father. He gets out of the car, walks around to the other side, straightens his tie, and opens the car door for your mother! And he says to her, "Shut up! Get over here and hold my arm. And smile, we're at church."

Maybe at church that day the pastor says to your dad, "Would you please come and share your testimony with us?" And your father gets up and gives his testimony about the day he became a believer when he was nine years old, and how he was a terrible sinner and came to meet Jesus Christ, and how everything changed. Then he says you need to meet Jesus Christ as your personal Savior, and you start to wonder how that's made a difference in his life.

You hear your father say, "This Bible is the most important book in my life. I live to read this book. I believe it has all the answers." And you're there thinking, "Can you believe this? Just listen to Dad! He never reads his Bible! When did it become so important?" When you get home, you watch him take this same Bible and set it on top of his dresser, where he never touches it all week. You hear him give flowery prayers at church, but he never prays like that at home. And pretty soon you say to yourself, "I know what church is all about. It's about people who fake it. They say the right things, and carry the right books, and sing the right songs, but there's nothing real inside of them." And before long, you find yourself sitting in the third chair. You look at the second chair, and you say, "The church is filled with hypocrites, and I want no part of it!"

Men, if you want to leave a lasting legacy of first-chair children, you are going to have to move to the first chair. You can't stay in the second chair and leave a legacy of faith! You can't look the part, dress the part, act the part, but not live the part. You've got to be a man who says, "As for me and my house, we will serve the Lord."

Take a look at another family for a moment. In which of these three chairs would you put David? You'd have to put him in the first chair. He's a man after God's own heart. But watch his son Solomon, who comes on the scene as the wisest man who ever lived. Trace Solomon's life. In his early years, when he's young and tender before the Lord, God says, "What do you want? Of all the things in the world, what do you want, Solomon?" And the reply is "I want to be wise and rule the kingdom for You." Solomon sounds just like his father. But as he grows older, instead of choosing the way of the first chair, he permits his heart to grow cold.

That's what happens with many second-chair people. Their hearts start out hot when they're young, but then they cool a little bit, and a little bit more, and things begin to tragically transition from "God and me" to "me and God." Finally, inside the heart, where only God is supposed to dwell, there is an emptiness, a dryness, a disappointment, a sadness. "Is this all there is? There has to be more."

LIVING IN THE SECOND CHAIR

You can spot a second-chair person by looking at his values. When his faith starts getting colder, he starts going after money. Getting ahead in the world and having a better job in the world take precedence over being sold out to the Lord. The second-chair man works more and more hours to buy more and more things because that hollow feeling inside has not been filled by God Himself. Instead of the Word being the overwhelming authority in his life, the Bible is something he carries with him to church, sets down on Sunday afternoon, and yells each Sunday morning, "Who took my Bible?"

When you grow up in a home that moves away from putting God first, you become a person who is motivated by money and power and prestige. The first-chair person puts people first. The second-chair person put his own pleasure first. It's as though you moved from David to Solomon. David took a physical nation and made it into a spiritual nation. Then he gave it to Solomon, and he made it into a secular nation. Then Solomon gave it to his son Rehoboam, and the nation split—ruined in just three generations.

That first chair is focused on people. First-chair people love people because God loved people enough to die for them. The second chair is focused on possessions. These people love things because that's where their pleasure is derived.

Do you realize that the chair you're currently sitting in has a massive influence on everyone around you? Do you realize what you're doing to your children, and your grandchildren, and generations down the road? The choices you make today will influence them perhaps for eternity. If you aren't in the first chair already, it's time to move and to bring your children and grandchildren with you.

LEAVING A LEGACY

The first-chair person is sold out to the Scriptures and has submitted to the authority of God's Word. The Bible instructs him on what to do when he isn't sure. He doesn't go scrambling after everyone else's opinion. Instead, he approaches the Bible to determine God's will for his life, and submits to it. But a second-chair person simply owns a Bible. When something comes up and he tries to decide what to do, he won't go back to the Scriptures. Instead, he goes to his friends or perhaps asks another Christian. He makes his decision depending on what good Christian people say, not the Scriptures. And as our world becomes more and more anti-God, more and more sinful and rebellious to God Himself, those in the second chair start moving further away from the Lord and closer to the world. Their choice of music, television, books, even their very lifestyles reflect the world rather than God, because second-chair people ultimately follow the world's example rather than God's revelation.

For instance, go back ten or twenty years. If you had seen a movie that contained rough language or sexy situations, you'd have blushed. You would have thought to yourself, "I hope nobody sees me in here." Why? Because the conviction of your parents, and of the Word of God, is that those sorts of entertainment are improper. The Spirit would say to you, "Don't watch that. God doesn't want you in here. Get out of here." It would bother you. Your conscience would cause you to feel shame. But after you've seen untold numbers of movies of all types, some of them in your own living room, you eventually don't feel the same way about them. You figure, "If others are watching them, it's probably OK for me too." Rather than the values of Scripture being your practical authority, the values of other Christians become your authority. And, as the polls verify, the behavior of believers is often not any different than that of people who fully reject God.

As a matter of fact, if you mention the certain inappropriate movie to people in the first chair and they criticize that sort of entertainment, their attitude bothers you. It offends you. Where is their tolerance? What business is it of theirs what you watch? "You're just too old-fashioned," you tell them. "You haven't kept up with the times."

You're right, of course. They haven't moved with the times, but you have. They've held firm to a lifestyle that honors God, and you've moved away from it.

This slide from commitment to compromise to confusion isn't new. This has been going on since the beginning of time. The apostle Paul once said to the believers at Corinth, "There are some among you who are spiritual." That's the first chair. "There are some among you who are natural." That's the third chair. They don't even know the Spirit of God. Then Paul said, in a sense, "Then there's the large number of you in the middle who are carnal. You are believers, but you've got one foot in the world and one foot in the church." That's the second chair. (See 1 Corinthians 2–3.)

First-chair men have a relationship with God that doesn't just take place on Sundays. It's real. It's honest. They walk with the Lord daily. Second-chair men start out with a relationship that's real and vital, but unless they move to the first chair, they soon see worship as just another responsibility. Pleasure becomes the focus of their lives. Their faith is dry and empty. "I know I should read the Bible," second-chair men complain. "I just don't have time." They try to get to know God from guilt. Christian, God wants *you*. That's all He wants. And when you find God in that first chair, you're going to find your heart singing. You're going to find yourself living your faith in front of your children on a daily basis so that they'll see your honest, vibrant relationship with the Lord. You'll leave a legacy of God's power in your own life.

MOVING TO THE FIRST CHAIR

Well, where are you? In Revelation chapter three, Jesus Christ speaks about these three chairs and says, "I know your works, that you are neither cold (that's third chair) nor hot (that's the first chair). I wish that you were either cold or hot. So then because you are lukewarm (that's the second chair), it makes me so frustrated I could spit you out" (see 3:14–16).

Now look at verse 17, and you'll see what the problem is with the middle chair: "Because you say, 'I am rich, have become wealthy, and have need of nothing,'—and do not know that you are wretched, miserable, poor, blind, and naked—I counsel you to buy from Me gold" (NKJV). God wants you to get real gold, not the fool's gold. If you're in the second chair and think you've got it made, you have committed your life to a mirage. You think you're rich, but you're poor. You think you've got it made, but you've got nothing.

Now look at verse 19. You might not know it, but this is how God feels about a man in the second chair: "as many as I love…" God *loves* a man wherever he sits, but He has a word for the man in the second chair. "As many as I love," He says, "I rebuke." Get out of the second chair, brother. God is rebuking you.

Next He says, "Be zealous!" God says, "With all the passion, all the commitment, all the drive in your heart, get out of the chair!" Be zealous! Be a man and get out of that second chair. He doesn't tell us to think about it; He says, "Do it! Just do it!"

Verse 20 is for a second-chair person. We use it when we talk to people who don't know Jesus Christ, and it's acceptable to apply it that way, but you must understand that this passage is not talking to the believer who's in the first chair or to nonbelievers in the third chair. This verse is speaking directly to those in the second chair. He says, "Behold, I stand at the door and knock." He's knocking on a believer's heart. He's already *in* this man's heart. This man already knows the Lord as His personal Savior. He knows about the works, but he just doesn't live with or for God. "Behold, I stand at the door and knock. If anyone hears My voice and opens the door, *I will come in to him and dine with him, and he with Me*" (NKJV, emphasis mine). Notice that Christ doesn't say, "I will come in and save him." Why not? Because this man is already saved! If you're in the second chair, your need isn't to know Christ; your need is to let Christ *rule your life!* That's the need of the second chair.

It's my observation that too many second-chair Christians have secretly given up believing they can ever really walk with God. But Christ is saying, "I've already saved you. Now will you let Me rule your life? Will you repent and move to the first chair?"

I want you to know, I used to be in the second chair. I probably know more about it than you do. It's not fun. But God wants second-chair Christians to change. He loves you. He rebukes you. And He is waiting for you to get up and move to the first chair.

Repent. Be zealous. Say to the Lord, "God, I'm sorry for the second chair in my life. Forgive me. I don't want to be here anymore. I don't want to do that to my kids anymore. I don't want the emptiness anymore. I'm going to pick up my chair and walk right over to that first chair. Why? Because, "As for me and my house, we will *serve* the Lord!"

STUDY QUESTIONS

1. What feelings do you have after reading this chapter? Explain.

2. Which statement best describes your family: 1) "We know God"; 2) "We know about God"; or 3) "We don't know God." Why did you choose the statement you did?

3. Consider your typical actions around the house. What do those actions reveal about what you value in life? About your commitment to God?

4. Define "legacy." What kind of "faith legacy" do you want to leave for your children? How can you pass on that legacy?

5. In your opinion, what is the best advice for fathers found in this chapter? Why?

6. Describe a time when you felt confident God was active in your life. How did that affect you?

7. Finish this sentence: "As a result of reading and discussing this chapter, one thing I'll do differently tomorrow is..."

CHAPTER TEN

SETTING AN EXAMPLE

JOHN MAXWELL

I'll never forget the time I was getting ready to speak to seventy thousand men at a Promise Keepers conference. I was in a room all by myself with my Bible, preparing for what I was about to share, when the worship leader asked everyone to get into groups for prayer. Since I had no group, I felt all alone. So I started to pray that my sixteen-year-old son, Joel Porter, could pray with me. Not two minutes later the door to the room opened and in walked my boy! The highlight of that conference was not the singing, or the speakers, or sharing encouragement with thousands of men. It was this father having a time of prayer with his son. To be completely honest, I could have left right then, because after that, everything else was going to be downhill.

As a father, I want to pass on a heritage to my son, a heritage he can pass on to his kids, a heritage like the one passed on to me. I'm a third-generation preacher. My dad is a prayer warrior and a man of integrity. Right before I was to speak at that conference, Dad had a heart attack, so I flew across the country to Orlando to see him. I walked into his hospital room just before they were to take him into surgery and opened my Bible to Psalm 101:6. And I read the words of the psalmist, which paraphrased say: "The integrity of your life has been a ministry unto me."

I looked at my father that day and said, "Dad, the integrity of your life—not that you were a great pastor, not that you were a church planter—the integrity of your life is what has been a ministry to me." We prayed together, and then they wheeled him out.

We had some good moments together over the next five or six days. But one day things became so tough the doctors weren't sure he would make it. My brother, who is a couple of years older than I am, got some oil, and we went into the room and laid hands on our father as James teaches, and we anointed his head with oil and prayed over him.

My two children, Elizabeth and Joel Porter, and my wife, Margaret, had also flown out to Orlando to be with him—just in case. I'll always remember the scene in that hospital room—JP on one side of the bed, Elizabeth on the other, and my father holding their hands and praying over them just as Jacob had prayed over his children. I sat there with Margaret, holding her hand and saying to myself, "What an incredible heritage I have. What a godly heritage I have been blessed with."

Every man wants to be able to pass on that kind of a heritage to his son or daughter for the next generation, and the next generation, and the one after that. Every man wants to leave a legacy of godliness for his children to imitate.

The day before I was to leave for the conference, I told my dad how disappointed I was that he wouldn't be able to hear me preach to those Promise Keepers men. "Son," he said, "I can't be with you, but why don't you take my Bible and preach out of it?

Then it will be almost like I'm there." Later, as I flipped through his Bible on the plane, I found every page of it marked. He had studied that book thoroughly and had even marked the times he had read through the Bible, with the date he started and the date he ended. I counted that he had read through that Bible thirty-eight times!

Holding the Word he had read so often and looking at the notes and the dates he had written, I felt like a rookie. I felt as if I had never really read the Word. I looked at that Bible and said, "God, help me to be a man of the Word like my father." More than anything else, I want to be a man of the Word and set an example for my children as my father set for me.

ATTITUDE AND ACTION

I believe we can all become godly examples for our families, and to do so we need to remember two words. The first is *attitude*. We need to have a teachable attitude when we come to God's Word. The second word is *action*. We ought to have obedience that leads to action. When we can put those two words together, when we have an attitude of teachability and we back it up with an obedient walk, God's Word can beautifully change our lives.

Recently I've been studying the life of Samson. Here was a man appointed by God to be a leader of the children of Israel, a Nazirite anointed from birth, set aside to lead Israel out of bondage to the Philistines. The Bible says he was blessed by God as he grew up. Yet, when you look at the end of Samson's life, you find him in prison, grinding at a wheel, blind. He is not the man God intended him to be. He is not the man God ordained him to be.

I look at Samson and ask myself, "What happened?" I've read Judges 13–16 many times, and my conclusion is that he lost his teachability. He no longer had a teachable spirit, and teachability is key in becoming a man of God.

SEEK GOD'S WISDOM

Four things happened in Samson's life that can happen in our lives if we lose that teachable spirit. First, when we're no longer teachable, we lean on our own strength and understanding rather than seeking God. We begin to rely on our own wisdom instead of the Lord's.

That is exactly what happened in Samson's life. We know he was a strong man, a big guy with muscles, the kind who worked out at the gym all the time. We see him manhandling lions, grabbing foxes, and defeating the Philistines.

But we can also sense a spiritual change in his life. In the fifteenth chapter of Judges, Samson begins to assess what has happened. He reflects on his strengths and starts saying things like "*I've* made donkeys out of them. *I've* killed my enemies." He starts being more concerned with "what I have done" than what the Lord wants. He no longer is thinking about his example, but himself. A man who was born with an anointing now has become a man of arrogance. He has lost his teachable spirit.

When Mohammed Ali was the heavyweight champion of the world, he was on a plane one day. As it was preparing to take off, the flight attendant noticed he hadn't fastened his seat belt. "Mr.

Ali," she told him, "you need to fasten your seat belt." He looked at her and said, "Superman don't need no seat belt." She looked right back at him and said, "Superman don't need no airplane either. Buckle up."

Solomon said, "Trust in the LORD with all your heart, and lean not on your own understanding; in all your ways acknowledge Him, and He shall direct your paths" (Proverbs 3:5–6, NKJV). If you want to set an example for others to follow, you're going to have to rely on the wisdom of God over your own wisdom. The Lord Jesus told us, "Without Me you can do nothing" (John 15:5, NKJV). I used to look at that passage of Scripture and think, "What does He mean, without Him we can do nothing? We can do a lot of things without Jesus. Then one day it hit me: Without Him we can do nothing of *eternal value*. Everything I do without Jesus is wood, hay, and stubble. The moment I allow Him to work through me, I begin to do things that have eternal consequences and permanent value.

LEARN FROM YOUR MISTAKES

The second thing that happens when we lose our teachability is that we fail to learn from our mistakes. You can look at Samson's life and see history repeat itself. He was continually being deceived by women. His wife deceived him, a prostitute deceived him, and eventually Delilah mortally deceived him. Why did he keep falling into the same traps? Why didn't he learn from his mistakes?

Just because a mistake is obvious doesn't mean we'll learn

from it. I once watched a hockey goalie being interviewed on television, who said, "How would you like to have a job where every time you make a mistake, a big red light goes on and eighteen thousand people boo?" Samson excelled in making great big mistakes. I once heard that "a mistake is only a failure if you never learn from it." If so, then Samson was a failure for much of his life because he made big mistakes, over and over again.

Portia Nelson wrote the world's shortest autobiography, and it's all about learning from mistakes. It goes like this:

Chapter One: I walk down the street. There's a deep hole in the sidewalk. I fall in. I'm lost. I'm helpless. It isn't my fault, and it takes forever to find my way out.

Chapter Two: I walk down the same street. There's a deep hole in the sidewalk. I pretend I don't see it. I fall in again. I can't believe I'm in the same place. But, it isn't my fault. It still takes a long time to get out.

Chapter Three: I walk down the same street. There's a deep hole in the sidewalk. I see it is there. I still fall in. It's a habit. My eyes are open. I know where I am. It is my fault, and I get out immediately.

Chapter Four: I walk down the same street. There's a deep hole in the sidewalk. I walk around it.

Chapter Five: I walk down another street.[1]

Because Samson lacked a teachable spirit, he leaned on his own strength instead of God's, and he never learned from his mistakes.

As Solomon put it in Proverbs 10:17, "He who heeds discipline shows the way to life, but whoever ignores correction leads others astray." Rather than setting an example of godliness, his lack of teachability set an example of error.

LEAD RATHER THAN REACT

The third evidence that we lack teachability is that we react instead of lead. That was true of Samson. Instead of leading the people out of bondage to the Philistines, he constantly reacted to them. For example, when the Philistines coaxed his wife into discovering and revealing the answer to his riddle in Judges 14, Samson blamed others. When he learned his wife had been given to another man in chapter 15, Samson said, "Now I will really harm them." After his wife was killed by angry Philistines, Samson declared, "Since you've acted like this, I won't stop until I get my revenge on you."

Those are all *reactions,* not positive *actions.* A leader is in trouble when he flies into a rage or gets defensive. He's in trouble when he passes the buck. He's headed for trouble when he doesn't listen to people. And there is danger ahead when a leader has personal problems. All these things describe Samson. Anointed and appointed by God to be a leader, Samson lost his teachability because he wouldn't listen to the Lord or keep a humble spirit before Him.

This man was supposed to be setting an example for others to follow. As a leader, he should have been carefully planning his actions. Instead, he spent all his time and energy on *re*actions. He was always on the defensive, always worried about what some-body else was doing. A godly man is proactive in setting an example, not reactive. Rather than being concerned with what his *opponents* are doing, his first concern is what his *God* is doing.

AVOID TEMPTATION

The fourth thing that happens when we lose our teachability is that we yield to temptation. Look at what Samson did. Rather than staying away from the Philistines, as God told him to do, Samson dated their women and hung out with their men. He started to compromise. Delilah kept asking him the secret of his immense strength, hoping to get the truth so she could destroy him.

> With such nagging she prodded him day after day until he was tired to death.
>
> So he told her everything. "No razor has ever been used on my head," he said, "because I have been a Nazirite set apart to God since birth. If my head were shaved, my strength would leave me, and I would become as weak as any other man."
>
> When Delilah saw that he had told her everything, she sent word to the rulers of the Philistines, "Come back once more; he has told me everything." So the rulers of the Philistines returned with the silver in their hands. Having put him to sleep on her lap, she called a man to shave off the seven braids of his hair, and so began to subdue him. And his strength left him.

Then she called, "Samson, the Philistines are upon you!"

He awoke from his sleep and thought, "I'll go out as before and shake myself free." But he did not know that the LORD had left him.

Then the Philistines seized him, gouged out his eyes and took him down to Gaza. Binding him with bronze shackles, they set him to grinding in the prison." (Judges 16:16–21)

Those are some of the saddest words in Scripture. Samson thought he could escape his sin one more time. He had always been able to before, but this time he didn't know the Lord had left him. He was deceived by his seductress, and it cost him his leadership role. God had prepared Samson for leadership in special ways, but Samson's own pride and sin hindered God's plan.

One reason I want to be a man of God's Word is so that when the evil one comes, I will have God's Word hidden in my heart and I will not be deceived. I don't want to wake up one morning to realize I missed the best that God has for me because I became careless and lost my teachability.

ALL THAT WE CAN BE

When I look at the story of Samson, three things grip my heart. First, sin will always take us farther than we want to go. Nobody ever intends to go too far into sin, but they get carried away by their actions. Before they know it, they are deep in sin, and any thought of setting a godly example is gone. Sin always takes us farther than we want to go. It took Samson all the way to destruction.

Second, sin will always keep us longer than we intended to stay. The evil one wants to trap us in sin so he can destroy us. We fool ourselves into thinking sin doesn't have consequences, that we can sin for a while, then give it up and be godly. But sin saps us of our strength and our character. When Samson got up from Delilah's bed to flee, he found that all his strength was gone.

And third, sin will always cost us more than we are willing to pay. Samson didn't intend for his sexual sin to cost him his power and position, but it did. Many men who become involved in sexual sin fail to realize its cost until it's too late—and too expensive. It costs them their wives, their families, their careers, and sometimes their lives. For all, it costs their reputation and example. Sin has a price, and it *will* be paid one day.

I can picture Samson at the end of his life—a man whose parents the angels visited before his birth to say, "He will be a leader, an example. He is anointed." But the only thing Samson was leading late in life was the handle of the millstone. He became an example to Israel, but not the way God desired. Blind and in shackles, Samson was an example of what happens to a man who rejects the Lord's leading to follow his own path. Instead of taking the role God designed for him, Samson was stuck in the role he created for himself. He lacked a teachable spirit, and it cost him everything.

Christian, I believe this is your hour. God is moving in the lives of men. His purpose—to make you a leader, a man of integrity, a man of holiness, a man who loves his wife and kids. To grow into that, you must have a teachable spirit and a heart for the Word of God. That's our calling, and there is no shortcut to it. If you want to set an example, you are going to have to put God's Word into practice.

What I have found is that many of us know the Word of God, but we lack obedience to it. We go to church, hear sermon after sermon, but are educated way above the level of our obedience. We are not only to read God's Word, but we are to hide it in our hearts and become obedient to it. It's time we begin taking our faith seriously and get some spiritual exercise by putting what we know into action.

When I go to the Word of God, I don't examine it. It examines me. Instead of looking into Scripture, the Scripture looks into me. What I really want in my life is for the Word of God to take up residence inside of me so that I become Christlike. I want the Word of God to come into my heart and change my life. Colossians 3:2 says that I am to set my mind on things above, and that's what happens when Scripture gets inside of a person.

It's so easy for us to get trapped by earthly things, to get sidetracked by the temptations and concerns of this life. But through the Bible, the Lord can help us put to death the things of the earthly nature—the immorality and impurity—and raise to life a new man, equipped and ready for leadership in his home and in the world.

No matter what has happened in the past, you can become a

man of God's Word. You can be an example to your children, as my father was to me, and as I have tried to be to Elizabeth and Joel Porter.

As I mentioned, my father wasn't able to go with me to Promise Keepers that day because he was in the hospital. But as I was getting ready to leave him to catch a plane to the conference, I sat down and talked with him. He asked me, "What time will you be preaching, John?"

"Two o'clock on Saturday afternoon," I said.

"That's fine, Son. That's when I'll be praying for you." And I knew he would because he has always been a man of the Word, and a man of his word.

In the future, I would like your children to be able to say the same thing about you. Commit yourself today to being teachable. And dedicate yourself to being a man of God's Word. Make that decision. And someday down the road, your children will look you in the eye and be able to say, "I know what my father stands for—God and integrity." What an awesome legacy that will be, not only for them, but for their children who will follow them.

[1] Source unknown.

STUDY QUESTIONS

1. Who has been the best example of godliness to you? How has that impacted the way you live?

2. In what ways are you like Samson? How does that make you feel?

3. Tell about the *best* mistake you ever made. What did you learn from that experience that made it so worthwhile for you?

4. Why is it valuable for a leader to be proactive? How can you be proactive in the leadership of your family?

5. When are you tempted to compromise God's standards? How can we help each other overcome those temptations?

6. True or False: "A godly example doesn't come from wanting to be an example, but from wanting to be godly." Explain your answer.

7. When, like Samson, have you felt the cruel effects of sin in your life? How might a teachable spirit help you when sin threatens your life during the coming week?

CHAPTER ELEVEN

KEEPING AN OPEN HAND

RON BLUE

I am not a preacher, nor am I an economist. I am not even a forecaster. There are only two kinds of economic forecasters: those who don't know what's going to happen, and those who don't know that they don't know what's going to happen.

Neither am I a tax expert. The only thing I know is that I have been on this earth for fifty-five years, and April 15 occurs every year. I've looked at my calendar, and April 15 is there again, which means that we'll owe taxes again next April. Of course, the problem is not taxes; the problem is that we don't prepare and plan for April 15.

You also ought to know that I am not an investment expert. When people ask me, "Should I buy or sell my stock?" I say, "Well, if it's going to go up, I'd buy it. If it's going to go down, I'd sell it." You would be amazed how much people pay me for that kind of advice!

Finally, I'm not a prophet. The risk is too great. In the Old Testament, if a prophet was wrong, he was stoned to death, so I've never applied for the position.

What I am is a businessman, though I used to be a drug addict, of a sort. My drugs were wealth, position, money, power, and all of those things that tend to drive men.

Then in 1972 my wife came home after suffering a very serious illness, getting involved in a Bible study, and accepting Christ as her Savior, and said to me, "I've become a Christian." My inner response was "Good. It'll probably help her, and that will help our marriage." Because if anything was wrong, it was probably her fault. That was an arrogant attitude, but I suspect many feel the same way.

Two years later, after watching her live out the reality of Jesus Christ in her life, I couldn't explain away her changed life. And on my way to play golf one day, I pulled out the Four Spiritual Laws, read through them, and prayed the prayer. I said, "God, I'm willing to be changed from the inside, but I don't intend to change anything of my own will." He took me seriously. That day I shot a thirty-six on the front side, and I thought, "If I'd have known this, I'd have become a Christian a long time ago!"

Then God began to change my life. Three years after committing my life to Christ, Judy and I got on our knees and told the Lord that we would be willing to go anywhere or do anything to follow Him. At the time I owned a C.P.A. firm and two little banks. At one time I had the smallest bank in the state of Indiana, the Poland State Bank. (I always considered myself an international banker!) Yet God took us seriously and literally moved us out of Indianapolis and brought us to Atlanta, Georgia, where over the last several years we have been helping people throughout this country plan and manage their finances according to biblical principles.

THE PROBLEM OF PERSPECTIVE

What I have found is that individuals and families in America have a big problem with their perspective about money. We are filled with fear, confusion, doubt, and uncertainty. Why? One reason is our past mistakes. Statistically, 80 percent of Americans have more debt than they have assets. That's the bad news. The good news is that they don't know it! They've never added up all that they own and all that they owe and compared the two. Most of us, then, have made some serious mistakes. As a matter of fact, the reason I've written six books is that I've made enough mistakes to fill six books!

The second thing that gives us fear, confusion, doubt, and uncertainty is advertising. For example, when I hear the slogan, "You deserve a break today," I always want to say, "Who says? Who says I deserve a break today?" Or, "You only go around once. Grab all the gusto you can get." We have bought into a philosophy of "We owe it to ourselves."

A third contributor to our fear and confusion about our finances is economic uncertainty. When I turned fifty in 1992, I was concerned about where our country was going. Larry Burkett had just written a book called *The Coming Economic Earthquake*, and I was concerned that by 1995 we would be in serious trouble. I asked God, "Lord, what's going to happen?" He didn't tell me, but He did say, "Look back." I looked back to 1982, when I turned forty, and we had 17 percent interest rates. We had an oil crisis. We had high inflation. I said, "Well, age forty wasn't any good. I'm going back to thirty." I went back to when

I was thirty in 1972. We had an oil embargo in 1972. The prime rate hit 10 percent for the first time. Many of us businessmen wondered if we would survive. I thought to myself, "Well, that's not getting any better. What about when I turned twenty in 1962?" I was in college at Indiana University at the time, and I remember watching television in the basement in the fraternity house as Nikita Kruschev banged his shoe on the table, saying, "We will bury you." And I remember thinking, "There may not even be a world for me to graduate into." So I went back to when I was ten in 1952, in Lafayette, Indiana, and what I remember about 1952 was that bomb shelters were big sellers. As a matter of fact, they turned the courthouse in Tippecanoe County into a bomb shelter that housed thirty-five thousand people. I remember the 1950s as a time of great fear. Then I went back to when I was born. That was 1942, right after Pearl Harbor, and I suspect there wasn't a lot of certainty, economically or politically, in 1942.

So here's the lesson: Economic uncertainty is certain. It isn't going to change. It isn't going to be better one year, two years, three years, four years, five years from now, or ten years from now. So if you're waiting for things to be better or different before you get a hold on your finances, you'll wait forever.

We have poor advice even from our leaders. I testified before a congressional subcommittee a few years ago. And as I sat there with the senators on the podium and the television cameras were on, a senator asked me, "Mr. Blue, can you tell me what you would tell the American family relative to their finances?"

And I thought to myself, "This is the most ridiculous thing I'm going to say to this man. They're going to laugh me right out of this senate caucus room." But I took a deep breath and said, "Well, senator, I would say four things to the American family. Number one, spend less than you earn. I know it's un-American, but spend less than you earn. Number two, avoid the use of debt. Number three, build liquidity into your financial situation. And number four, set some long-term goals so you have an idea where you're going." I thought, "This is ridiculous. These people are going to laugh."

Then the senator said to me, "Wait a minute, let me get these down." And he says to me, "Spend less than you earn."

I said, "That's right."

"Avoid the use of debt."

"Correct."

"Maintain liquidity?"

"Uh-huh."

"Set long-term goals."

"That's right, Senator."

And then he said, "You know, it seems to me that would work at any income level."

"You're right, Senator," I told him, "including the United States government."

Think about it. If as a nation we decided to live within our income, not borrow, maintain liquidity, and had some idea about where we were going, we would be financially secure. And it wouldn't make a difference whether we had inflation, deflation, economic uncertainty, or whatever. It's not an issue of a new technique. These principles are timeless, based on biblical wisdom.

THREE QUESTIONS

Each of us has three legitimate questions regarding money:

First, "Will I ever have enough?"

Second, "Will it continue to be enough if I ever do have enough?"

And third, "By the way, how much is enough?"

Someone once asked Wayne Gretzky, "How is it that you're such a great hockey player?" And he made an incredible statement: "It's because I don't skate to where the puck is; I skate to where the puck is going to be."

We would like to do the same thing economically. We would like to figure out where the economy is headed so we could get there ahead of time. But, as the Chinese proverb says: "Forecasting is very difficult, especially about the future."

The Bible doesn't give us that kind of answer. But I'd like to draw some perspectives on finances from God's Word as we look for answers to those three questions.

GOD OWNS IT ALL

In Matthew 25:14 we read: "For it is just like a man about to go on a journey, who called his own slaves, and entrusted his possessions to them" (NASB).

The word *it* refers to the kingdom of heaven. Jesus is saying, "I'm going away, and I'm going to come back, and this is what it's like." He says, "I'm going to entrust my possessions to them." The bottom line of financial management, the bottom line of financial planning, the bottom line of stewardship is very, very simple: God owns it all. It's not my part and your part. It's all His. That's the perspective we need to take from Scripture.

Consider the implications. First of all, the owner has all the rights, and the trustee or the steward has only responsibilities. He has no rights. I remember when my daughter turned sixteen and I entrusted my car to her for the first time. I understood the difference between ownership and stewardship. It was my car, and I expected it to be returned in a particular condition, with gas in it, at a particular time. And I had the right to do that because it was my car. If you believe that God owns it all, that means, number one, He can take whatever He wants whenever He wants. It's His. I hold whatever He has entrusted to me with an open hand.

Let me share with you a story about a couple named "Mr. and Mrs. Thing":

Mr. and Mrs. Thing are a very pleasant and successful couple, at least that's the verdict of most people who tend to measure success with a thingometer. When the thingometer is put to work in the life of Mr. and Mrs. Thing, the result is startling. There he is, sitting down on a very luxurious and expensive thing, almost hidden by a large number of other things. Things to sit on, things to sit at, things to cook on, things to eat from. All shiny and new. Things, things, things. Things to clean with, things to wash with, things to clean and things to wash. Things to amuse, things to give pleasure, things to watch, and things to play. Things for the long, hot summer and things for the short, cold winter. Things for the big thing in which they live, and things for the garden, and things for the lounge, and things for the kitchen, and things for the bedroom. And things on four wheels, things on two wheels, and things to put on top of the thing on four wheels, and things to pull behind the four wheels, and things to add to the interior of the thing on four wheels. Things, things, things, and there in the middle are Mr. and Mrs. Thing, smiling, pleased as pink with their things, thinking of more things to add to their things, secure in their castle of things.

Well, I just want you to know that your things can't last. They're going to pass. There's going to be an end to them. Maybe an error in judgment, maybe a temporary loss of concentration, or maybe you'll just pass them off to the second-hand thing dealer. Or maybe they'll wind up a mass of mangled metal being towed off to the thing yard. And what about all the things in your house? Well, it's time for bed. Put out the cat. Make sure you lock the door to make sure some thing-taker doesn't come and take your things. And that's the way life goes, doesn't it? And someday when you die, they only put one thing in the box. You.[1]

I don't know the answer to the question of how much is enough, but I know the answer to the question of how much is too much. "Too much" is whenever I take what God has entrusted to me and close my hands. Whenever I take over what's His, I have gone from being a steward to being an owner. Biblically, my possessions actually belong to God. You've never seen a hearse pulling a U-Haul, and you never will.

Second, if you believe God owns it all, then every spending decision you make is a spiritual decision. There is nothing more spiritual about tithing than there is about taking a vacation, if all that you have belongs to God. I didn't say it's wrong to take a vacation, but when you consider that He owns everything, then every decision you make is a spiritual decision.

Third, you can't fake stewardship. In fact, it's the only area of the Christian life you can't fake. You can fake prayer. You can fake a good relationship with your wife. You can fake anything except how you handle His resources, because your checkbook reveals it. Your checkbook writes the story of your trusteeship. It's the bottom line of integrity. If you take His resources, and you use them for His purposes, that's stewardship. I have a client who said it this way: "I got saved in 1960, and my pocketbook got saved in 1962."

THE GROWTH PROCESS

"And to one he gave five talents, to another, two, and to another, one, each according to his own ability; and he went on his journey. Immediately the one who had received the five talents went and traded with them, and gained five more talents. In the same manner the one who had received the two talents gained two more. But he who received the one talent went away and dug in the ground, and hid his master's money. Now after a long time the master of those slaves came and settled accounts with them." (Matthew 25:15–19, NASB)

When is Jesus coming back? I don't know. But it sure seems like He's been gone a long time, and it says in the Bible that after some time He's going to come back, and He's going to settle accounts. Now, what happens to us is we tend to forget He's coming back. We tend to forget we're going to die, and over time we slowly assume "ownership." We lose sight of the first principle: that God owns it all.

But the Lord goes on in His story and says:

"Now after a long time the master of those slaves came and settled accounts with them. And the one who had received the five talents came up and brought five more talents, saying, 'Master, you entrusted five talents to me; see, I have gained five more talents.' His master said to him, 'Well done, good and faithful slave; you were faithful with a few things, I will put you in charge of many things; enter into the joy of your master.'" (vv. 19–21, NASB)

The second principle is that we are in a growth process. Jesus says, "You were faithful with a few things, now I will put you in charge of many things. Enter into the joy of your master." How many things is He going to put us in charge of? I don't know. But I do know this: Currently the wealthiest man in the world is the Sultan of Brunei, who has fifty billion dollars of personal wealth. But you know what? Fifty billion dollars probably couldn't buy downtown Atlanta. And my God owns downtown Atlanta. My God owns the state of Georgia. My God owns all fifty states. My God owns the world. That's the perspective. Even the wealthiest person in the world owns only a few things. But God says, "I will put you in charge of many things."

Let me give you an idea of the spiritual perspective on God's laws of compounding. If I gave you $10,000 and you were able to invest it at 25 percent, at the end of forty years you would have $75 million. That's enough to retire on! If you were only able to earn 24 percent, you would have $54 million instead of $75 million, a difference of $21 million. One percentage point difference. If, under God's laws of compounding, I put to work His resources, and they produce thirtyfold, fiftyfold, and a hundredfold, they have grown spiritually at the rate of 3,000 percent, 6,000 percent, and 10,000 percent respectively. How much is a $100 investment at 10,000 percent for all eternity? That's the perspective He wants us to have. He says, "Look, I've given you a few things. Use them faithfully, and then I'll put you in charge of things that you can't even comprehend. Enter into the joy of your master."

It's interesting to see what happens with each servant.

"The one also who had received the two talents came up and said, 'Master, you entrusted to me two talents; see, I have gained two more talents.' His master said to him, 'Well done, good and faithful slave; you were faithful with a few things, I will put you in charge of many things; enter into the joy of your master.'" (vv. 22–23, NASB)

What's different about what he said to the one who had two talents as opposed to the one who had five talents? If you look at the scripture, you'll see the words of the master are identical. In other words, *the amount is irrelevant*. It's not important. You don't become a steward; you already are a steward. It's not when you get to a particular point. *You are already there*. You are now a steward. And it doesn't make a difference whether you have a lot or a little. He's the One who is responsible for entrusting it to you, and He's the One who will reward you for how well you handle His property.

BELIEF DETERMINES BEHAVIOR

"And the one also who had received the one talent came up and said, 'Master, I knew you to be a hard man, reaping where you did not sow, and gathering where you scattered no seed. And I was afraid, and went away and hid your talent in the ground; see, you have what is yours.'" (vv. 24–25, NASB)

Here's an important point: Belief determines behavior. It says the unfaithful servant was afraid. What was he afraid of? Was he afraid of ridicule? Was he afraid of losing it? Was he afraid of the master? Or was he just plain fearful? I don't know the answer to the question, but I do know this: Scripture shows that when we become fearful, we tend to do less. And I believe that one of Satan's traps is to create fear, confusion, doubt, and uncertainty.

Statistically, we know this: As fear and uncertainty increase, giving goes down. As a matter of fact, in America in the last fifteen years, incomes have gone up five times, and among evangelicals giving has gone down by almost a third. We are the most prosperous nation in the world. Eighty percent of evangelical wealth in the world is in America, and we've lived through the last fifteen years, the most prosperous time this country and this world have ever seen, and giving among evangelicals has gone down. I believe it's because of fear.

Do you remember the twelve spies who went into the land? They ran into the Amalekites, and the Hittites, and the Jebusites, and the mosquito bites, and all those "ites" that were in the land. And they said, "We saw the sons of Anak there, and we were afraid" (see Numbers 13:27–31). Ten out of twelve were afraid to go into the land. They were afraid to take possession of what God had given them. It's the same way in the American church today. Ten out of twelve of us are scared to death, and as a consequence we don't use the resources entrusted to us because we are driven by fear rather than faith.

"But his master answered and said to him, 'You wicked, lazy slave, you knew that I reap where I did not sow, and gather where I scattered no seed. Then you ought to have put my money in the bank, and on my arrival I would have received my money back with interest.'" (vv. 26–27, NASB)

In other words, *put it to use*. There are only five things you can do with money. You can give it away. You can pay your taxes. You can pay off debt. You can save it. Or you can spend it. How you allocate it among those five things depends upon your goals, values, and priorities, and they come out of God's Word. That's what becoming a man of integrity is all about—setting and changing values, priorities, and goals.

So the master in the story says, "Therefore take away the talent from him, and give it to the one who has the ten talents" (v. 28). Why did he give it to the one with the ten talents, instead of the one who had the four talents? Why did he take it away? I don't know the answer. But I don't have to know the answer because I know He's the owner. He can do with it whatever He wants to do. He can take whatever He wants, and He can give it to whomever He wants, whenever He wants. *And He's going to give it to those who are faithful in their use of it*.

> "For to everyone who has shall more be given, and he shall have an abundance; but from the one who does not have, even what he does have shall be taken away. And cast out the worthless slave into the outer darkness; in

that place there shall be weeping and gnashing of teeth."
(vv. 29–30, NASB)

Here is the bottom line: Jesus is coming back, there is a heaven and a hell, there is a judgment, and there are rewards for how we handle His resources. How we spend eternity, if I interpret this passage correctly, is somehow determined by how we use the resources God has entrusted to us.

HOLDING WITH AN OPEN HAND

So, what are the answers to the three questions?

First, "Will I ever have enough?"

The answer is "Absolutely." Your source is the Lord. He knows what you need when you need it.

Second, "Will it continue to be enough?"

You bet.

"But what if we have an inflationary blowout or a deflationary collapse?"

Do you think God is sitting in heaven right now, worrying, "How's it going to turn out in America?" Do you think God's wringing His hands, looking over the ramparts of heaven, saying, "I sure hope they make it in America"? I don't think so. "Will it continue to be enough?" Absolutely.

And third, "How much is enough?"

That you have to answer for yourself. And the answer to that question can be found by looking at your "finish lines." What's your lifestyle finish line? How much is enough to satisfy you in your lifestyle? I can guarantee that if you're looking for either security or significance, you can't accumulate enough to be either secure or significant. What's your finish line on accumulation, on lifestyle, on debt, and on giving?

Christian, hold everything He gives you with an open hand. I don't understand how much is enough, but I understand how much is too much, and I think the greatest threat facing America today is not poverty but prosperity. Adlai Stevenson once said, "If I wanted to bring a nation to its knees, I would give it so much that it became miserable, greedy, and sick." Our responsibility is to hold whatever God gives us with an open hand. If He chooses to give us a lot more, that's fine. But getting more will never, ever meet a need. We have the potential, I believe, to change the world economically and technologically. God's not worried, and my encouragement is, don't miss the miracle of being obedient to what He wants to do in your life.

[1] Author unknown

STUDY QUESTIONS

1. In your own words, how would you summarize the message of this chapter?

2. The four biblical principles of managing your money are: 1) spend less than you earn; 2) avoid the use of debt; 3) maintain liquidity; and 4) set long-term goals. When applied, which of these principles would make the greatest impact on your family's finances right now? Why?

3. When it comes to financial resources, how much would you say is "enough" for your family?

4. Reread the parable of the talents (Matthew 25:14–30). What questions come to your mind after reading this parable? How would you answer those questions?

5. If the statement "God owns everything" is true, how does that affect the way you and your family use finances?

6. What do you think God expects of you when it comes to your financial resources?

7. What makes it easy or difficult for you and your wife to discuss the family's finances? What can you do this week to improve that communication?

CHAPTER TWELVE

CHANGING THE WORLD

CHUCK COLSON

More than anything else, our country needs committed Christian men at this moment. A couple of years ago there was a proposal for welfare reform in Washington, D.C., a bill called "The Personal Responsibility Act." Can you think of anything sillier than the Congress of the United States being able to pass a law to create personal responsibility? Personal responsibility is created when men decide to keep their promises to God, and to their families, and to their country. That's what brings personal responsibility to America, not what the Congress does.

We can gather as men from every background, but we are one in Christ, responsible to love one another. It doesn't make any difference if you're black or white, rich or poor, in prison or free. You may be Catholic or Protestant, Baptist or Lutheran or Presbyterian. If I belong to Jesus and you belong to Jesus, we belong to each other.

Now the fact of the matter is that things are getting a little better. There used to be a lot more hostility between denominations than there is today.

Just a few years ago Patty and I were in Northern Ireland, where for years there has been open warfare between Protestants and Catholics. While we were there, a bishop in the Anglican church took a ride on a Sunday afternoon down one of the rock-walled country roads in beautiful, green Northern Ireland. As he was coming around a bend, he was thinking about his sermon that morning, and he wasn't paying any attention to his driving. Coming around the bend the other way was another car, and the two of them collided right in the middle of the road. Out of the other car stumbled a Catholic priest. The Anglican bishop ran up to the Catholic priest and said, "Father, I'm so sorry. It was my fault."

And the priest said, "No, it was entirely my fault. I wasn't looking where I was going." The two men stood in the middle of the road holding one another up. Finally, the priest said to the bishop, "You look a little shaken. I think I have something you need." He walked back to his car, opened up the glove compartment, and took out a pint of Irish whiskey. He brought it back to the bishop and said, "Here. Take a swig. It will steady your nerves."

The bishop looked around. No one was there. (He's an Anglican, not a Baptist.) And so he took a big swig, then he handed it back to the priest, saying, "Thank you, Father. That has really steadied my nerves. That is just what I needed. Isn't this wonderful? What an act of Christian love. Protestants and Catholics are fighting in Belfast, and here you share your whiskey with me. Thank you. Won't you have a drink with me?"

The priest looked at him and said, "No thank you. I think I'll wait until after the police have come."

THE WEAPONS OF GOD

Karl Barth, a great theologian of the twentieth century, said that every morning a Christian should wake up with a newspaper in one hand and the Bible in the other. Not that those two are equal, mind you. One is totally reliable, the other is hardly reliable at all. But the Christian should always look at what is happening in the world in the light of what God's Word says. That means, as Christians we are to take every thought captive in obedience to Christ. We are to look at what's happening in the world and judge it by what God says.

Do that today, and you can't help but become a little discouraged. You find ethical collapse on every front. Family breakups. Crime. Violent crime is up 560 percent since the 1960s. Pornography. Violence. Disrespect for law. And the shocking, unconscionable taking of unborn lives every year in the name of choice.

I was with my good friend Bill Bennett, former Secretary of Education, having lunch and talking about history and philosophy and politics and lots of things of interest. The conversation was lively and animated, and about fifteen minutes into it, Bill looked at me and asked, "Chuck, can you tell me one thing that is getting better in America today?" There was a twenty-second pause as I groped for an answer. Bill laughed and said, "I ask the same thing of all my friends. Nobody has a good answer."

I believe there is a war going on between two distinct worldviews. At the heart of that war is a question—"Is there truth?" And you see, the reason you and I are in the gun sights is that the world believes in unfettered autonomy as the ultimate goal of life, so it views anyone who says, "There *is* truth, an absolute standard," as an enemy. It isn't so much that they're persecuting us; it's that what we stand for is the one barrier against liberty being turned into license.

That's why those who write about the Christian men's movement don't understand what we're doing. That's why they say in the *Washington Post*, "It's a misogynistic movement." My goodness, whatever a misogynistic movement is, if it gets men back to loving their wives and families, we need more misogynistic movements! That's why they say men's meetings are a cover for right-wing political activities, because they can't think of anything else to say. They don't understand it, and they don't want to understand it.

Cultural elites have gone to such ridiculous absurdities as the Salt Lake City judge who ruled that "The Lord Bless Us and Keep Us" couldn't be sung at a junior high school commencement. The reason they couldn't sing it was that the word *Lord* is in the song. It had been a tradition, but for the first time in years and years, they weren't allowed to sing it. So at the commencement a young man went up to the platform, took the microphone, and said to the crowd, "Let's just spontaneously sing." And they all sang "The Lord Bless Us and Keep Us." Then police came and took the man off the platform and arrested him. The world is afraid even of the *name* of God.

I have to tell you honestly that the old, carnal Chuck Colson comes out when I see stuff like this. I start getting mad. The old marine captain, the old White House hatchet man, starts think-ing, "It's about time we fought back and put those bigots in their place!" That's what we all want to do. But that's not God's way.

What is God's way? What's God's weapon? "The world will know that you're My disciples by your... politics"? No. "...by your theological conferences"? No. "...by your denominations and your doctrines"? No. "...by how hard you can fight back"? No. "The world will know you're My disciples by your love for one another" (see John 13:35).

THE POWER OF LOVE

The love of the body of Christ is the most powerful weapon God has to change this society. There was a time less than two thou-sand years ago that Christians were used as human torches. They were lighted by Nero to entertain at his parties. Christians were thrown into the lions' den. The apostle Paul wrote a message to the church and said, "Overcome evil with good" (Romans 12:21). Let the world see the love of Christ. That's what the incarnation is! God has overcome the evil of the world by bringing His perfect, sinless Son to die on the cross for the sins of mankind and thereby to restore man to peace with God.

We make a terrible mistake in America today if we think we're going to win this culture back by our political movements. Now, politics are important. We should be involved in politics, fighting for the rights of the unborn and for justice and against some of the ridiculous, absurd things that are being done in this country. We have to be fighting for them politically. We also have to be making a powerful apologetic defense of truth in our culture. We have to be engaged with this culture. But ultimately, nothing we do will make any difference unless it flows out of the body of Christ—men and women committed to a genuine *koinonia* of love for one another. We'll never be able to accomplish anything in America unless we *are* the people of God. Then God will use us to do His work.

I suspect nobody else alive knows more of the power of love than I do. Twenty-four years ago I was in the midst of Watergate. You couldn't pick up a newspaper in America without reading about what a bad guy Chuck Colson was. Every day it was on the television. Then I met a man, and what so impressed me was that he loved me, no matter what. And one night, in the driveway of his home, in a flood of tears, I called out and said, "God, take me, just the way I am." My life has never been the same, and never can it be again.

Soon after my commitment, some friends arranged for me to meet a few other Christians. Sitting across the room was a great big bear of a man named Harold Hughes, a liberal Democratic senator from Iowa. Let me tell you, if you want to talk about being poles apart, take Chuck Colson, Nixon aide and conservative Republican from the East, and place him across the room from a liberal Democratic senator from Iowa. I slowly told the story of my conversion and my acceptance of Christ. About halfway through, this big, burly guy, who used to be a truck driver and an alcoholic, stood up and said, "I've heard enough." And he started across the room toward me. I don't mind telling you I was a little nervous. He's a big guy. He reached down, picked me up, and said, "I believe Jesus Christ has come into your life, and therefore we are brothers, and I will stand with you." And so he did, all through Watergate. Two people who were absolute political poles apart, drawn together by the love of Christ. And that's what overcomes this world.

In some ways the defining moment of my Christian life came after I was in prison seven months. I'd been part of that little prayer group, and they used to come to prison to meet with me. They stuck with me, even when I was the most reviled man in America, when I was going through trials, and when I was being attacked by everyone. In January 1975 in prison, I hit my low point. I learned that my son, who was in college, had been arrested for drug possession. I was in prison. My son was in jail, and I couldn't reach out to him. I learned I was disbarred in one state. My dad, my closest friend, had died. My mother was alone. My wife was having difficulty managing things. The other three guys in Watergate, who were in prison with me, were released because they'd been sentenced by another judge.

About that time I received a phone call from Al Quie, seventh ranking Republican in the House of Representatives. He said, "Chuck, we've been praying, and we've been hurting for you because of what you're going through. I found an old pre-Civil War statute that says one man can serve another man's prison sentence, and I'm going down tomorrow to ask President Ford if I can come in and serve your sentence so you can go home."

As I went to bed that night, in my little bunk in that prison,

I got down on the dirty floor and said, "God, thank You, because now I know the truth." *Greater love has no one than this, that he lay down his life for his friends* (John 15:13). That's the gospel. And it's true. I saw it lived out. And it is what the world is desperately, desperately hungering for.

NO GREATER LOVE

When I received the Templeton Prize a few years ago, I was in Chicago, and I agreed to do an interview for a special program on PBS. The interview was set up in the Blackstone Hotel in an old, smoke-filled room where the politicians used to meet. After the camera equipment was all set up, the woman interviewer started asking me questions. She looked kind of tough, like she'd been through some hard things in her life. Behind her plastered pancake makeup were a lot of creases and lines, and a look of pain registered in her eyes. She asked me, "How can you be so sure, Mr. Colson, about the reality of God?"

I said, "Because when I was in prison, Al Quie offered to come in and serve my prison sentence." And I began to tell her the story. Seconds into that story, I saw tears running down her face. She waved at the cameras to stop, and she got up and went out and made herself up again. When she returned, she said, "We'll film that scene again." So she asked the question all over again, and I answered it again. I looked over the second time, and again tears were rolling down her cheeks. But this time she didn't bother to stop the cameras.

Afterwards I talked to her. A Methodist, she hadn't been in

church in twenty years. She had a tough background, a broken family. She said nobody was really her friend. But she told me the story had touched her at the deepest level, and she would read my book, and she would get back to church.

You see, the world is desperate to believe what Jesus said. They are aching to see brothers and sisters who love one another and who are truly bound together in the love of God. The world can't resist that. That love will overcome the world where nothing else will ever do it. That is the great power of the Christian church.

If you don't think that will overcome the differences in this world, let me tell you about an experience in Northern Ireland not so many years ago. In the McGilligan Prison, where many political prisoners are held, there was a man by the name of Jimmy Gibson, an Ulster defense terrorist. He used to kill Catholics for fun. But in a Bible study with Prison Fellowship one night, Jimmy Gibson gave his life to Christ. He was dramatically transformed.

That prison happened to have apartheid. On one side lived the Catholics, on the other side the Protestants. They never crossed the dividing line. There was no interaction between Protestants and Catholics in that prison. Jimmy Gibson got up one night at dinner in the mess hall, and he walked across the mess hall and found an empty seat at random among the Catholic prisoners.

He sat down by a guy named Liam McCloskey and leaned over and said, "Brother, I want to tell you about Jesus." That whole mess hall went silent. People expected a riot. The guards went after their guns. But those two brothers sat there and talked. And

Jimmy Gibson, over those next weeks, ate every night with the Catholic prisoners. In time, he led Liam McCloskey to Christ.

In 1983 I was at Queens College in Belfast, Northern Ireland, with eleven hundred people in the crowd—Protestants and Catholics, the first time they'd come together. Jimmy Gibson walked up to the platform on one side, Liam McCloskey came up the other, and they threw their arms around one another. And Liam looked at the crowd and said, "Two years ago on the street I would have killed this man. Today he's my brother in Christ. I will lay down my life for him."

Brother, that's the secret. That's the power: love.

THE EXPERIENCE OF LOVE

How do we experience this? I think there are three ways.

First, get into a small accountability group. One of the most important things in my Christian life has been a small group of men to whom I'm accountable. I won't make any major decisions in the ministry of Prison Fellowship without consulting them, and they have to give me unanimous support. I hold myself accountable because I don't trust myself.

Second, belong to a local church. I don't mean "belong" by just going Sunday morning and getting your ears tickled. I mean belong to a church where the Word of God is preached, where the sacraments or ordinances are observed, where discipline is exercised, where there is a genuine *koinonia*, and where you participate in being equipped to go out and live the gospel in the world. That's what church is all about, and you can't live the

Christian life if you aren't serious about your commitment to the church. John Calvin was right. You cannot experience a conversion—a transformation—outside of the church.

Third, you've got to recognize that you are part of the universal fellowship. To all those whom God has regenerated, all those for whom Jesus has become Lord of their lives, who hold to the ancient creeds and the confessions, and who believe the authority of Scripture and believe in Jesus alone for their salvation, I extend the right hand of fellowship because my heart beats as their hearts beat.

We are to be part of an accountability group, part of a church, and part of the universal body of Christ. And from that, the love of God begins to flow out of us into the world. And the world will be drawn to Him.

In Prison Fellowship we have something called Angel Tree, which is closer to my heart than anything else. Through it, last year we distributed Christmas gifts to 430,000 kids in this country, kids who have a mommy or daddy in prison. We brought them gospel comic books, we brought them an illustrated Bible, and we witnessed to them about Jesus. Every year Patty and I do it, and I love it. It flows very naturally out of our love for one another. The principal love we have is a love for one another, but out of that flows a love for the world.

Christmas before last, the Church of God in Waterloo, Oregon, adopted a family. When they went to deliver the gifts, they found that the mother was a prostitute on drugs, the father was in prison, and there were three little kids—a five-year-old boy, a three-year-old girl, and a two-year-old boy. They brought them into the church and had a party. Those little kids were thrilled because people were loving them, perhaps for the first time in their lives. After the church gave the kids the gifts, the pastor of that small church, who was sitting in his study preparing his sermon, heard a knock on the door. He opened it, and there were the three kids. "Mister, would you show us around your church?" the five-year-old asked. So the pastor picked up the two-year-old, and the others followed as he showed them around. And he said to them, "Any time you'd like to come back, please come."

The pastor went back to preparing his sermon, and fifteen minutes later there was another knock at the door. He answered it. The three kids again. "Mister," the five-year-old said, "can we come to your church if we don't have any socks?" And the pastor said, "Of course. Why do you ask?" And the little boy told him, "My little brother doesn't have any socks, but can we come to your church anyway?" The pastor said, "Service will be in an hour. You come this morning." At nine o'clock that morning, three little kids walked into that church carrying a brown paper bag with a hot dog in it because they didn't know how long church would last. And they sat there in the midst of that fellowship, and they were loved by the people in that church, and that family was saved because the love of God spilled out into the community.

That's exactly what should happen to the church. The world will knock on the door and say, "Mister, tell us about your church" when they see our love. That's what will change American culture.

KEEPING YOUR PROMISE

It's easy to make promises about how we'll love others, but how do we keep them? As I look back over the last twenty-four years, I think about what God has done in my life. I've written twelve books, many of which have won awards and honors. I've spoken in the Parliament. I've gone to Buckingham Palace for the Templeton Prize. I've received all kinds of wonderful things, so I could just sit back and rejoice at the way God has taken our ministry and spread it to seventy-five countries around the world.

But when I sit down and reflect on what God has done for me, you know what I appreciate the most? I think most about the fact that Jesus Christ, the Son of God, went to a cross, was nailed to it, and died there in payment of my sins so that the stuff in my heart is removed, and I can live free. Because it's a fact: He died for me on that cross. That's the single most important thing in my life. The Son of God, sinless, died that I might be free. It has to fill you with awe. If you really are a Christian, if you really understand what it means, it has to fill you with an overwhelming sense of awe and gratitude to God. God loved me. How can I repay Him?

I've been in seven hundred prisons in forty-nine countries. I was in prison this morning, and I loved it. It was great to see men coming to know Christ. Of course, the prisons are rotten holes. I've been in places in South America where you slip on the sewage coming out of the cells. I've been in prisons in Zambia where the men haven't anything to wear or eat, and your heart breaks. People say to me, "Why do you keep doing this? Why do you keep going back and back and back to these prisons?" I do it because it is my duty, out of gratitude to God, for what He has done in my life. I can do nothing else! The only way you keep a promise is to understand the gratitude you owe to God Almighty for sending His Son in order to take your sins away. And out of gratitude, you do your duty. You keep your promise.

Let me give you an example of duty. I happened to pick up a prayer by a man whom I admire greatly. John McCain is now a United States Senator from Arizona, but when I was in the White House, he was a prisoner of war. His father, Admiral Jack McCain, was a great friend of mine. My heart used to break because my friend's son was locked up in the Hanoi Hilton. Little did I know the prayer he prayed while he was in there. It was printed in *Life* magazine:

> The way we got into prison wasn't because of God. It was because we were rendering unto Caesar what was Caesar's, because our countries were at war. It wasn't right to ask God to free me, though. I thought I should leave that situation only if it were in the best interests of my country. In 1968 the Vietnamese offered me the opportunity to go home. I had a broken arm, a knee I couldn't walk on without crutches, and I weighed about a hundred pounds. I wanted to go home more than almost anything in the world. But our code of conduct says the sick and injured go home in order of their capture, and there were others who had been there longer. I knew they wanted to

release me because my father was commander of US forces in the Pacific. It would have given them a propaganda victory. I prayed for the strength to make the right decision, and I'm certain those prayers helped me do what I had to do. I had to stay there.

John McCain did his duty to his country, even though it meant he had to stay in that cell for seven years as a shriveled-up body of a hundred pounds. But it was his duty, out of gratitude for what the founders of this country did and the people who have given their lives that we might have freedom. He took an oath and he honored it.

Brothers, how much greater is our gratitude for Him who went to the cross and died for our sins that we might be free? Therefore we should have the sense of duty that says, "I will do the right thing no matter what, even if it results in my suffering, even if it results in my hurt. I will do my duty." I pray we might be a people who will do our duty, loving one another that the world will know we are His disciples.

"Oh, Father, I pray," Jesus said, "that they may be one with one another, as I am one with You, and I in them, and You in Me, in order that the world would know that Thou didst send Me" (see John 17:20–23). If you are not at one with your brothers, you are preventing the world from knowing that Jesus came. It is a pre-condition to evangelism. It is the heart of the Christian life. May God make us that kind of people.

STUDY QUESTIONS

1. Can you think of one thing that's getting better in America today? Why or why not?

2. Why do you suppose love can be such a powerful weapon in the battle to change our society?

3. When have you experienced the power of love in a meaningful, life-changing way?

4. How can a man's involvement in an accountability group and in a local church help him experience the power of God's love?

5. Reread the story on pages 189–90 about the Church of God in Waterloo, Oregon. What can we learn about expressing God's love from that story?

6. What's one promise of God that you find most comforting? How is God's love expressed in that promise?

7. What's one promise of love that you'd like to make to those in your sphere of influence (including family, friends, coworkers)? How will you express that loving promise this week?

CHAPTER THIRTEEN

THE POWER OF A PROMISE KEPT

HOWARD HENDRICKS

The event of the year was the high school play in a sleepy, West Texas town. Unfortunately, the young man playing the lead role was miscast. At the climax of the scene, the hero was to go down on his knees before this beautiful young lady and propose to her. At that point the window was to go up, the jilted suitor was to fire the gun, and the lead man was to leap to his feet frantically and shout, "Good heavens, I'm shot!" It looked plain and simple on the page, and that's just about the way he would say it. The poor kid would deliver the line in a complete monotone. They coached and drilled him, but the kid had no histrionic abilities whatever. He just could not identify with the part.

The night of the high school play, as the drama coach was going out the front door, he noticed his son's air rifle in the corner. And he got an idea. Sure enough, at the critical point, with the hero down on his knees before the beautiful young lady, the window going up, and the jilted suitor firing his gun, that coach, with split-second timing and accuracy, pulled the trigger of the air rifle off stage, nicking the kid's trousers. The kid stole the show, leaping to his feet and crying, "Good heavens! I AM shot!"

THE NEED FOR INTEGRITY

America's need is much the same as that of the young actor—a need for authenticity. Credible and trustworthy leaders are fast becoming an endangered species. Wherever I go across America or around the world, the screaming need is for leaders who keep their word. We need leaders in our homes. Families are unraveling like cheap sweaters. Marriages are exploding like firecrackers on the Fourth of July. We need leaders in our churches. *Leadership* magazine did an extensive survey and discovered that 85 percent of the churches in America are in trouble. They have either plateaued or they are in serious decline. We need leaders in our society. The landscape is littered with men and women leaders who have sold their souls for a mess of materialistic pottage.

The greatest crisis in America today is a crisis of leadership. And the greatest peril of leadership is a crisis of character. Think about it, to give a person management techniques and leadership skills without integrity is simply to enable him to become a better rip-off artist. A book appeared some time ago entitled *The Day America Told the Truth*, and that was the day America blushed. Peter Kamm and James Patterson did an extensive study of all fifty states. They included younger people, older people, men and women, people of all races and economic backgrounds. And they discovered a disturbing truth. Only 13 percent of Americans consider all Ten Commandments as binding and relevant. Most Americans lie regularly to their families, to their friends, and to their associates. Americans admit goofing off at work an average of seven hours a week. One half of our work force regularly calls in sick, though they admit they feel perfectly well.

Here's the clincher. When asked, "What are you willing to do for $10 million?" 25 percent of those surveyed said they would abandon their families. Twenty-three percent said they would engage in prostitution for a week. Seven percent said they would commit murder! Superficially I concluded, "But...but that represents the thinking and lifestyle of pagans." Wrong. Doug Sherman, together with my son Bill, wrote a book entitled *Keeping Your Ethical Edge Sharp*. Their conclusion was that Christians are as likely as non-Christians to falsify income tax returns, to plagiarize printed materials, to bribe someone in order to obtain a building permit, to ignore construction specs, to shift the blame for wrongdoing onto someone else, to illegally copy a computer program, or to steal from the workplace.

I've never forgotten the story of a man who left the factory every day with a pile of sand in his wheelbarrow. The guards went through the pile, convinced they would find stolen property, but they could find nothing. Every day, same thing. Finally they realized he was stealing wheelbarrows. In the United States, we have come to a place where our citizens selectively obey the laws of the land, doing whatever is most convenient and expedient for us, bending and breaking the laws. As a born-again Christian, that ought to drain the blood right out of your system.

It is transparent to any thinking individual that the greatest need of our times is the need for integrity. It's not optional; it's an urgent requirement. We need a core of men of whom it can be said, "What you see is what you get. No phony baloney." A storm center of men who not only promise but, more importantly, perform. Men of their word. What they say is what they do. They are who they are, no matter where they are or with whom they are.

BECOMING A MAN OF INTEGRITY

I'd like to ask you three questions. First, what does it take to be a man of integrity? How do you get a handle on that? Begin by looking at your dictionary. What does Webster say? His insights are incredible. He defines integrity as an "unimpaired or unmarred condition; soundness; uncompromising adherence to a code of moral, artistic or other values; utter sincerity, honesty and candor; avoidance of deception, expediency, or shallowness of any kind; complete and undivided." A man of integrity has nothing to hide. He has nothing to fear. He has nothing to prove. And he has nothing to lose except his wholeness and honesty.

What does Scripture have to say about this kind of man? Consider some selected passages which I believe build a convincing case that God is into character, not credentials. God told Solomon, in 1 Kings 9:4–5, "As for you, if you walk before me in integrity of heart and uprightness, as David your father did, and do all I command and observe my decrees and laws, I will establish your royal throne over Israel forever." David understood correctly in 1 Chronicles 29:17: "I know, my God, that you test the heart and are pleased with integrity." Job, answering one of his sorry counselors, says in verse 5 of chapter 27, "I will never admit you are in the right; till I die, I will not deny my integrity." David invited God in Psalm 7:8, "Judge me, O LORD, according to my righteousness, according to my integrity."

Several proverbs underscore the same truth. Proverbs 10:9 reads, "The man of integrity walks securely, but he who takes crooked paths will be found out." Proverbs 11:3 says, "The integrity of the upright guides them, but the unfaithful are destroyed by their duplicity." Proverbs 20:7, one of my favorites, reads, "The righteous man walks in his integrity; his children are blessed after him" (NKJV). The greatest contribution you can make to your children is to model integrity. How seldom do I find young people today who, when asked whom they would like to be like, say, "I'd like to be like my father."

I met a kid in a barbershop one day and asked him, "Son, who do you want to be like when you grow up?" He said, "Mister, I ain't found nobody I want to be like." You think he's an exception? Then you are totally out of touch with this generation. This is a generation in which the pedestals are bare and young people are screaming for adults who are authentic.

Proverbs 29:10 warns that "bloodthirsty men hate a man of integrity and seek to kill the upright." Are you on that wanted list? Do you have the guts to stand alone? Do you pay your bills, your taxes? On time?

I love a letter that was sent to the Internal Revenue Service. The man wrote, "I haven't been able to sleep because last year in filling out my income tax form, I deliberately misrepresented my income. Enclosed is a check for $150. If I still can't sleep, I'll send you the rest."

Have you ever asked yourself the question, "If *60 Minutes* sent a crew to my office, would I be embarrassed by what they discovered?" A man of integrity has nothing to fear. Because of the consistency and the congruence in his life, examinations do not embarrass him.

WHAT DOES INTEGRITY LOOK LIKE?

The second question I want to discuss is "What does integrity look like?" I believe integrity is best defined and illustrated in a person's life—convincingly transmitted through what others see, hear, and feel in the heartbeat of a lifestyle. Joseph and Daniel are two examples from Scripture, a younger man and an older man, both of whom were men of integrity. If I could clone only two men to live in our generation that's about to enter the year 2000, I would select these two men.

The first, Joseph, was a model of trust. Genesis 37 recounts how Joseph was sold into slavery by his brothers. He was taken to Egypt, where, like cream, he rose to the top. The reason: Three times in chapter 39 you will read, "The Lord was with Joseph." The Lord gave him success in everything he did. In fact, Genesis 39:4 says Joseph found favor in Potiphar's eyes and became his right-hand man. This captain of Pharaoh's guard put Joseph in charge of his household and entrusted everything he owned to his care. The blessing of the Lord was on everything Potiphar had, primarily because of this man of integrity.

Enter the enemy. Beginning at the end of verse 6 we read, "Now Joseph was well-built and handsome, and after a while his master's wife took notice of Joseph and said, 'Come to bed with me!' But he refused. 'With me in charge,' he told her, 'my master does not concern himself with anything in the house; everything he owns he has entrusted to my care. No one is greater in this house than I am. My master has withheld nothing from me except you, because you are his wife."

Here was a man who had such team commitment that he wouldn't let his boss down in a crisis. And we need to remind ourselves that Joseph was probably in his late teens, at a time when his hormones were racing.

A student came up to me some years ago after class and said, "Prof, I don't know why you keep talking about getting involved with women. Women are not my problem."

"Well," I said, "sit down. You've got another problem!"

Joseph had a commitment, and he wasn't going back on his commitment.

But there was a second reason Joseph remained pure. Not only was he a man of commitment, he was also a man of character. So he asked Potiphar's wife, "How then could I do such a wicked thing?"

I thank God for a pagan father. My pagan father communicated nothing to me spiritually because he had nothing to communicate, and you cannot impart what you do not possess. But my father was a moral man. He taught me the importance of self-concept. And I can remember his saying to me over and over and over again, "Son, that's beneath you. Either change your name or change your behavior." Joseph was a guy who understood himself and understood that God had created him in His image.

Joseph asked, "How could I do such a wicked thing and sin against God?" He had conviction...commitment...character. These are the same tent pegs that secure us from the real temptations we face every single day in the marketplace. The essence of leadership is trust. If people trust you, they will follow you. If no one is following you, as E. V. Hill has said on a number of occasions, then, man, you're just out taking a walk. Here was Joseph, willing to forfeit his freedom so that he wouldn't compromise his conviction. We know that because the result of his decision was imprisonment. Moral purity is not something you hope to have; it's something you *choose* to have. Can your wife trust you? Can your children trust you?

I recently was privy to a most agonizing experience. An eighteen-year-old boy dressed down his father, who had run away from a twenty-eight-year marriage so he could shack up with some little dolly. I can still hear his excoriating words: "Dad, I cannot believe you could be so stupid and let your family down like this!"

Can your family trust you? Can your company have total confidence in you? I believe that whether you're an employee or an employer, you ought to be the very best employee or the most trusted employer it's possible to be in the sphere of influence where God has placed you. Joseph was a man who could be trusted.

There's a second man I want you to see. His name is Daniel, and his story is found in the book named after him. You need to remind yourself that Daniel rose to the top of three administrations. When

I was a boy, I went to Sunday school and heard the story of Daniel in the lions' den. You may remember it as I do, that Daniel was usually presented as an early adolescent, having the fresh-faced innocence of a young teen while surrounded by all those lions. It's a wonderful picture, but not biblically accurate. The guy was probably in his sixties, and some scholars believe he may have been in his seventies when he was cast into the den of lions!

King Darius, the Persian monarch, had an interesting pyramid in his organization. Darius was at the top, followed by three commissioners, a hundred and twenty satraps, and then all of the people below. The text tells us that Daniel began distinguishing himself among the commissioners and satraps because he possessed an extraordinary spirit, and the king planned to appoint him over the entire kingdom. He was going to be second in command.

So the jealous commissioners and satraps did a little underhanded investigation. Their conclusion: They could find no grounds for accusation, no evidence of corruption, impropriety, or negligence inasmuch as Daniel was competent, loyal, and totally clean. So they concluded, "We're not going to unearth anything. What we've got to do is examine his godly lifestyle." They came up with a plan to suggest to the king: "Let's issue an injunction that for thirty days anyone who makes a petition to any god or man besides you, O king, shall be cast into the lions' den." And the king thought, "That's a pretty good idea." (The king's royal ego was showing.) So they passed it, and as part of the law of the Medes and the Persians, once it was passed, it could not be changed, even by royal decree. Then the king discovered he had been sold down the river. The man he thoroughly trusted, the one he wanted to put second in command, was now the one to be cast into the lions' den.

What I want you to notice is that at sixty or seventy, when a lot of people are sliding for home, reaching for the bench, or at least talking about retirement, Daniel was still going full tilt. There are two lines to every man's life: a purpose line and a life line. The moment the purpose line begins to fall off, it's just a question of time before the life line goes too. But here was a man at the latter end of his life who had not lost his sense of purpose. He was an honest man, a man of integrity—not because it was convenient, not because it had a cheap price tag, but because that was his conviction.

Someone once asked me on a program, "If you had only one thing to give your four children, what would you give them?" I had thought a great deal about that, so I answered immediately, "Honesty." You show me a person who is honest with God, who is honest with other people, and, most of all, who is honest with himself, and I will show you a man of integrity.

Honesty is adherence to truth, and truth is always a return to reality. Unbelievers do not expect Christians to be perfect. (I hope you're not trying to pull that off.) Occasionally people come to me and say, "Hey, Hendricks. Would you recommend a church?" I always ask, "What kind of a church are you looking for?" After they give me the specifications, I say, "You're looking for a perfect church. I don't know of a church like that, but if you find one, don't join it because you'll ruin it."

John Gardner is one of my favorite writers, particularly his book entitled *Excellence*, in which he says, "The society that scorns excellence in plumbing, because plumbing is a humble activity, and honors philosophy because it is an exalted activity, will have neither good plumbing nor good philosophy. Neither its pipes nor its theories will hold water." In Colossians 3:17, Paul writes, "Whatever you do, whether in word or deed, do it all in the name of the Lord Jesus, giving thanks to God the Father through him." And again in verses 23–24: "Whatever you do, work at it with all your heart, as working for the Lord, not for men, since you know that you will receive an inheritance from the Lord as a reward. It is the Lord Christ you are serving."

I was flying out of Boston recently. The crew boarded the passengers and then got word that we'd have to get off because there was "a slight mechanical problem." So we all got off the plane, and they said, "In fifteen minutes you'll receive further information." You know how to tell the experienced travelers from the amateurs? The amateurs believe the public announcements. It was six hours before the plane finally took off for Dallas. The passengers were angry and impatient. And, as always happens, free drinks were freely offered. Well, there was a guy sitting across the aisle from me hotter than a hornet, and every time a flight attendant walked down the aisle, he would give her a portion of his mind he very obviously couldn't afford to lose. I thought, "The poor gal."

So after a while I walked back to the galley and talked to her. I said, "You know, I'm a frequent flyer, and I'm always looking for somebody doing a good job. American Airlines should be proud to have you on the team. I cannot believe how nicely you handled this obnoxious character sitting across from me."

She smiled and said, "Thank you very much."

Then I asked, "Could I have your name? I would like to write the company and tell them how much I appreciate you."

"Oh," she said, "I wouldn't. You need to know that I don't work for American Airlines."

"Oh, really?"

"No, I represent the Lord Jesus Christ."

So I picked myself up off the floor, and we had a delightful conversation.

How would you like to have someone like that working for you? That's what we need in America. Don't give me jazz about foreign countries being able to beat us. They're not beating us. We are defeating ourselves. We need a larger corps of guys who are men of integrity, who will penetrate the companies of the United States.

When I was talking on this subject some time ago, a dear guy came up, pulled out his handkerchief, and started blubbering. When I asked him what was the matter, he said, "I'm the only Christian in my company."

"You gotta be kidding!"

"Nope," he replied. "Just me."

"You mean to tell me you're the only believer in your whole organization?"

"That's right."

"Wow," I said to him. "Do you mean to tell me that God Almighty entrusted that entire outfit to you?"

Stop feeling sorry for yourself if you're the only believer on the block or in the tennis and health club. God has sovereignly placed you there as His representative of integrity.

IS IT WORTH IT?

There is a third and final question I want us to consider. What does integrity produce? Dr. Chuck Swindoll gives six answers, and each one shouts, "Plenty!" First, it produces the sustained cultivation of character. Integrity is long obedience in the same direction. Living in the midst of a cesspool society that cannot tell the difference between Chanel No. 5 and Sewer Gas No. 9, we need to cultivate reliable character.

Second, integrity offers the continual relief of a clear conscience. You can go home every day with a totally free and relaxed self-confidence.

Third, consider the personal delight of intimacy with God. There is no greater privilege than walking day by day with the Lord Jesus. I once brought a senior citizen of ninety-three years into my class. The old boy got up and said, "Guys, I'd just like you to know that for all but eight years of my life I've been walking with Jesus Christ." My students leaped to their feet and for almost ten minutes gave him a standing ovation. They cheered, they yelled, and later they said, "Prof, thanks for bringing in a man who has been walking with Jesus for that long. It's such a motivation in our young lives."

There's a fourth value, and that's the priceless gift of a lingering legacy. What will you be remembered for? Not for what you think. I used to believe my children would remember my messages. They don't. In fact, neither do I! I thought my kids would be impressed that I teach in a theological seminary. They aren't.

When my son Bill was young, he asked me one day, "Hey Dad, when're you going to get a new job?"

"What's the matter?" I asked. "You don't like my job?"

"Aw, it's not that," he replied. "It's just that I can't explain to anybody where you work. They all think you work in a cemetery."

What are you going to give your children? I suspect that most of us won't leave them a monetary fortune. I hope you don't feel sorry for yourself. I've spent time with some of the wealthiest people in this country who would give their right arm to get their kids back. They lived for the buck, and they accumulated big bucks, but they lost the most valuable things in their lives. I have officiated at a number of funerals, but I have never buried a man who, before he died, said to me, "Hendricks, I wish I had spent more time on my business."

A fifth benefit of integrity is the rare privilege of being a mentor. You have no idea of the fulfillment that could be yours if you would take on a younger man and help him build a solid foundation for his life. Long after you've gone home to heaven, that individual is going to be making tracks for Jesus Christ.

There is a sixth and final benefit from integrity, and that is the crowning reward of ending well—with no regrets. May I remind you that over half of the people who failed in the Bible failed in the last half of their lives. Whenever anybody asks me, "What can I pray for in terms of your life?" I will invariably say, "That I will finish well." I want to go home to heaven without embarrassment. I want to go home to meet God, realizing that I gave it my best shot and that I utilized the incredible resources God has provided for me in Jesus Christ. Are you ending well?

A PROMISE KEPT

Remember, it is not your past that will defeat you in your Christian life. Jesus Christ died for your past. You might have dropped the ball, and Satan is working you over like crazy, telling you that you will never amount to anything. You may even believe the little line, "The bird with the broken wing will never rise as high again." My friend, it may be beautiful poetry, but it's lousy theology. God always starts with you right where you are.

Now the ball is in your court. Will you keep your promises? Will you be a man of integrity? The choice is yours.

STUDY QUESTIONS

1. Do you agree or disagree with this statement: "The greatest crisis in America today is a crisis of leadership." Defend your answer.

2. If you had written this chapter, how would you have answered the question "What does it take to be a man of integrity?"

3. Joseph and Daniel are examples of integrity from the pages of history. Who have been examples of integrity in your lifetime?

4. Why do you suppose our society seems to have abandoned a commitment to integrity? What can you do about that?

5. Imagine you could "create" a man of integrity by combining any five qualities from people in history. Which qualities from which people would you choose to use?

6. What would it take to create a man of integrity in you?

7. What's one thing you've gained from reading this book that you want to be sure to remember in the months to come? How will you help yourself remember that?

AUTHORS

RON BLUE

Ron Blue is managing partner of Ronald Blue and Company in Atlanta, Georgia. Following his graduation from Indiana University with an M.B.A., Blue was with Peat, Marwick, Mitchell and Company for several years before founding his own C.P.A. firm, which grew to become one of the fifty largest in the country.

In 1977, Blue became administrative vice president of *Leadership Dynamics,* teaching biblically based management seminars in the United States and Africa. Convinced that Christians would better handle their personal finances if they were counseled from a biblical perspective, he founded Ronald Blue & Co., a fee-only financial planning firm, in 1979. Employing a staff of over 125 people, the company offers comprehensive financial planning, investment management, tax and business services to individual and corporate clients.

Blue is the author of six books on personal finances, including *Master Your Money,* a bestseller which is now in its twenty-first printing. He is also a columnist for *Home Life* magazine, has appeared on numerous radio and television programs, and is the host of the popular *Master Your Money* video series, which has been used in over five thousand churches across the country.

Blue currently serves on the Board of Directors for the Family Research Council, Campus Crusade for Christ, Promise Keepers, and the MacLellan Foundation.

Ron and Judy live in Atlanta and have five children and two grandchildren.

BILL BRIGHT

After receiving a bachelor's degree in economics, Bill Bright joined the faculty of Oklahoma State University. He later moved to Los Angeles, where he launched a successful business career. It was while living in California that Bright became a Christian, largely through the combined influence of his mother's prayers and a church he was attending. His intensive personal study of the Bible led him to formal seminary studies. Subsequently, he felt the call of God to share Christ with the students at UCLA. That activity soon became a full-time pursuit and gave birth to the worldwide ministry now known as Campus Crusade for Christ International.

From a small beginning in 1951, the organization now has more than 13,000 full-time staff and 101,000 trained volunteers in 161 countries. The area covered by Campus Crusade represents 98 percent of the world's population, and the ministry has grown to include more than forty special ministries to inner cities, prisons, families, the military, executives, athletes, women, men, and many others.

Bright has authored many books, articles, pamphlets, and booklets that have been distributed by the millions in most major language groups. Most recently, he was awarded the 1996 Templeton Prize for Progress in Religion. Bright also conceived the *Jesus* film, the most widely viewed film ever produced. It has been translated into 365 languages and viewed by more than 750 million people in 216 countries.

Bill is married to Vonette, and they have two adult children, both of whom are in full-time ministry.

CHUCK COLSON

Twenty-four years ago Chuck Colson was not thinking about reaching out to prison inmates or reforming the US penal system. In fact, this aide to President Richard Nixon was "incapable of humanitarian thoughts," according to the media of the midseventies. He was known as the White House "hatchet man," a man feared by even the most powerful politicos during his four years of service to President Nixon. He was sentenced for his involvement in Watergate-related activities and served seven months of a one- to three-year prison sentence. When news of Colson's conversion leaked to the press in 1973, the *Boston Globe* reported, "If Mr. Colson can repent of his sins, there just has to be hope for everybody."

Soon after his release, Colson and three friends launched Prison Fellowship, which today is one of the largest volunteer organizations in the world. Since that time, Colson has visited more than seven hundred prisons in forty countries and, with the help of nearly fifty thousand volunteers, has built Prison Fellowship into the world's largest prison outreach, serving the spiritual and practical needs of prisoners in seventy-five countries, including the US.

Colson has also founded Justice Fellowship, an organization dedicated to working with legislators and policymakers to enact restorative justice principles, and Neighbors Who Care, a community-based support system for victims of crime.

Colson received the prestigious Templeton Prize for Progress in Religion in 1993, which he accepted on behalf of Prison Fellowship.

Chuck and his wife, Patty, live in Washington, D.C.

JACK HAYFORD

What began for Dr. Jack Hayford as a temporary assignment to pastor eighteen people in 1969 has developed into a full-time senior pastorate. The Church on the Way in Van Nuys, California, now averages over eight thousand in weekly attendance, with a membership of more than nine thousand.

Hayford is recognized the world over for his commitment to practical application, resulting from insight into God's Word. He has been the guest on a wide variety of both secular and Christian radio and television programs, from James Dobson's *Focus on the Family* to Ted Koppel's *Prime Time*. Jack's own radio and television ministry, *Living Way Ministries*, reaches into more than two thousand communities in the US. It covers all fifty states and Washington, D.C., as well as Australia, Canada, New Zealand, Puerto Rico, and South Africa.

He has written more than five hundred songs and hymns, including the widely used song "Majesty," and serves on the boards of several Christian organizations, including Promise Keepers and the National Religious Broadcasters Association.

The author of more than two dozen books, among them *The Mary Miracle*, *Worship His Majesty*, and *Moments with Majesty*, Hayford also served as the general editor for *The Spirit-Filled Life Bible*, an accompanying Bible study series, and a Bible handbook. He is currently the senior editorial adviser for *Ministries Today* magazine.

Jack and his wife, Anna, have been married since their college days. They have four children (all married and in Christian ministry) and ten grandchildren (Jack says, "All bright and above average!").

HOWARD HENDRICKS

Dr. Howard Hendricks is a distinguished professor and lecturer at Dallas Theological Seminary. He is also chairman of the Center for Christian Leadership and a keynote speaker for Promise Keepers.

"Prof," as most people know him, serves on numerous ministry boards, including Promise Keepers, The Navigators, and Walk Thru the Bible. He has written or cowritten more than twenty books, including *Standing Together, As Iron Sharpens Iron,* and *Living by the Book.*

Howard and his wife, Jeanne, have four grown children and live in Dallas, Texas.

JOHN MAXWELL

Dr. John C. Maxwell is one of the top thinkers and equippers in the US in the areas of leadership, church growth, and personal development. He has over twenty-five years of experience in church and organizational leadership and was the senior pastor of one of America's largest churches for fourteen years.

In 1985 Maxwell founded INJOY, a Christian leadership organization dedicated to helping men and women reach their potential in ministry, business, and the family. Each month he impacts over 60,000 leaders through the INJOY Life Club and Maximum Impact personal growth lessons on audio cassette.

A creative, dynamic communicator, Maxwell speaks to over

250,000 people each year on topics such as leadership, personal growth, attitudes, relationship building, and Christian living. He is a regular speaker at Promise Keepers.

Maxwell is also the author of more than a dozen books with over half a million copies in print. His titles include *Developing the Leader within You, Developing the Leaders around You, Breakthrough Parenting, Partners in Prayer, The Winning Attitude, Living at the Next Level,* and *The Success Journey.*

His lifetime goals include equipping 100,000 pastors in leadership, raising up 1,000,000 lay people to pray for their pastors, and influencing 10,000,000 people through equipping churches. He considers his greatest asset his family and his greatest achievement getting Margaret to marry him.

To contact Maxwell concerning his itinerary or INJOY's products, call 1-800-333-6506.

BOB MOOREHEAD

Dr. Bob Moorehead has served as a senior pastor for forty years. In 1970, he became the pastor of a one-year-old church in Kirkland, Washington, which had a weekly attendance of seventy-five. Today, weekend attendance at Overlake Christian Church is more than sixty-five hundred at four services. Overlake has established eight daughter churches through the years, and a variety of special ministries.

Moorehead founded and is president of Northwest Graduate School of Ministry, which has a current enrollment of over two hundred graduate students. A new radio ministry, *Courageous*

Living, is heard daily nationwide, and he also hosts a weekly, one-hour talk show on a Seattle radio station called *This Week with Dr. Bob Moorehead.* In addition, he has authored twelve books and several other publications.

Bob and his wife, Glenita, have three adult children and eight grandchildren.

LUIS PALAU

Dr. Luis Palau was born in the province of Buenos Aires, Argentina, and committed his life to Jesus at age twelve. When he was eighteen, he began preaching on the weekends, and five years later he and several other young men organized a tent evangelism and radio ministry in Argentina.

In 1961, Palau joined Overseas Crusades International (now OC International) for ministry to Spanish-speaking people and later served as OC's Latin American Field Director.

The Luis Palau Evangelistic Association was founded in 1978, with international headquarters in Portland, Oregon. Palau is the author of forty-one books and booklets in both English and Spanish, as well as more than a hundred published articles.

Luis and his wife, Patricia, live in Portland, Oregon, and have four adult sons and five grandsons.

DENNIS RAINEY

Dennis Rainey is the executive director and cofounder of Family-Life, a division of Campus Crusade for Christ. He is the daily host of the nationally syndicated radio program *FamilyLife Today* and received the National Religious Broadcasters Radio Program Producer of the Year Award in 1995. In addition to being the senior editor of the HomeBuilders Couples Series®, a Bible study series for couples, he has overseen the rapid growth of FamilyLife Conferences on marriage and parenting.

Dennis and his wife, Barbara, wrote the best-selling *Building Your Mate's Self-Esteem*, which was re-released as *The New Building Your Mate's Self-Esteem*. One of their other books, *Moments Together for Couples*, has been on the Christian Bestsellers List for Clothbound Nonfiction. His latest book, *A Call to Family Reformation,* was released in 1996.

Dennis and Barbara have six children and live near Little Rock, Arkansas.

GARY SMALLEY

Gary Smalley is one of the country's best-known authors and speakers on family relationships. He is the author or coauthor of fourteen best-selling and award-winning books, along with several popular films and videos. He has spent more than thirty years learning, teaching, and counseling others, and has personally interviewed thousands of singles and couples, asking two questions: What is it that strengthens your relationships, and what is it that weakens them?

Combined, his books have sold close to four million copies. Several of them have been translated into other languages. *The Blessing* and *The Two Sides of Love* have won the Gold Medallion Award.

Over the past two years, Smalley has spoken to more than 500,000 people. His national informercial, "Hidden Keys to Loving Relationships," with Frank and Kathi Lee Gifford, has been shown to television audiences all over the world. This videotape series has been ordered by more than 750,000 people. For information about obtaining Smalley's videos or other marriage-building materials, call 1-800-84TODAY.

Gary and his wife, Norma, live in Branson, Missouri. They have three married children and two grandchildren.

JOE STOWELL

Dr. Joe Stowell is president of Moody Bible Institute in Chicago and a frequent speaker at churches and conferences throughout the United States and Canada. He writes regular columns in *Moody Magazine* and in *Today in the Word.* Stowell is heard daily on the broadcast *Proclaim* and weekly on the international radio broadcast *Moody Presents.* He has written a number of best-selling books.

Joe and his wife, Martie, live in Chicago and have three adult children.

BRUCE WILKINSON

Dr. Bruce H. Wilkinson is the founder and president of Walk Thru the Bible Ministries, an international publishing and training organization which exists to contribute to the spiritual growth of Christians worldwide through Bible teaching, tools, and training. More than five thousand Walk Thru the Old Testament and

Walk Thru the New Testament seminars are given each year across America, as well as in fifty countries and forty-two language groups around the world.

More than ninety million copies of Walk Thru's eight devotional magazines have been published, including *The Daily Walk, Family Walk,* and *Youth Walk.* Wilkinson serves as executive editor for many publications, has authored numerous books and courses, and has served as editor for several study Bibles. Additionally, he developed and is the featured speaker for *The 7 Laws of the Learner* and *Biblical Portrait of Marriage* video series.

Wilkinson serves as chairman of The CoMission, an international movement of more than eighty Christian organizations that have joined together to send hundreds of people for one-year terms to the former Soviet Union.

Bruce and his wife, Darlene, reside in Charlotte, North Carolina. They have three children—two married and one at home—and one grandchild.

RAVI ZACHARIAS

Ravi Zacharias has spoken in over fifty countries, including the Middle East, Vietnam, and Cambodia (during the military conflict), and in numerous universities worldwide, notably Harvard and Princeton. He has addressed writers of the peace accord in South Africa, President Fujimori's cabinet, the parliament in Peru, military officers at the Lenin Military Academy, and the Center for Geopolitical Strategy in Moscow. He is well versed in the disciplines of comparative religions, cults, and philosophy and held the chair of evangelism and contemporary thought at Alliance Theological Seminary for three and a half years.

Zacharias was born in India in 1946 and immigrated to Canada with his family twenty years later. While pursuing a career in business management, his interest in theology grew; subsequently, he pursued this study during his undergraduate education. He received his Masters of Divinity from Trinity Evangelical Divinity School. Mr. Zacharias has been honored by the conferring of a Doctor of Divinity degree from Houghton College and a Doctor of Laws degree from Asbury College.

Zacharias has been a visiting scholar at Cambridge University, where he authored his first book, *A Shattered Visage: The Real Face of Atheism.* His second book, *Can Man Live without God?*, was awarded a Gold Medallion in 1995 and has been translated into four languages. *Deliver Us from Evil: Restoring the Soul in a Disintegrating Culture* is the title of his third book, released in October 1996, with the accompanying video series to follow.

Zacharias is listed as a distinguished lecturer with the Staley Foundation. His radio program, *Let My People Think*, is broadcast on 256 stations nationwide, and he has appeared on CNN and other international broadcasts. He is president of Ravi Zacharias International Ministries, headquartered in Atlanta, Georgia, with additional offices in Canada and India.